D1093088

THE HIGHLAND
HIGH WAY

The Highland High Way

A High-Level Walking Route from Loch Lomond to Fort William

**Heather Connon
and Paul Roper**

MAINSTREAM
PUBLISHING

EDINBURGH AND LONDON

Copyright © Heather Connon and Paul Roper, 1996
All rights reserved
The moral right of the authors has been asserted

First published in 1996 by
MAINSTREAM PUBLISHING COMPANY (EDINBURGH) LTD
7 Albany Street
Edinburgh EH1 3UG

ISBN 1 85158 791 8

A CIP catalogue record for this book is available from the
British Library

Typeset in Stempel Garamond by Business Colorprint, Welshpool
Printed and bound in Great Britain by The Cromwell Press

Contents

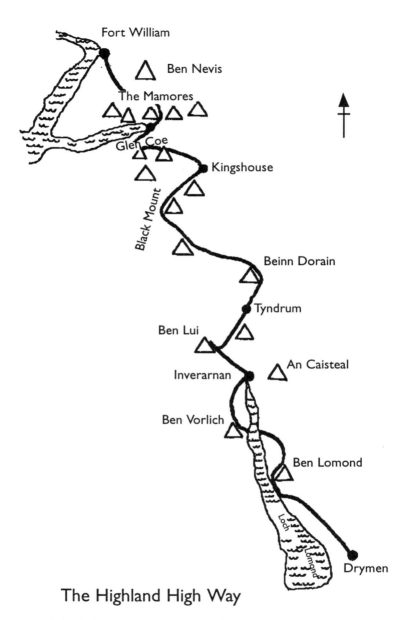

The Highland High Way

A high-level walking route from
Loch Lomond to Fort William

Introduction

The Highland High Way runs for 105 miles (170km) from Drymen at the south end of Loch Lomond north to Fort William.

On its way, it passes through some of Scotland's most spectacular scenery, goes round its most beautiful lochs and across its best-loved hills. Among the many highlights are Loch Lomond, justly famous for its lush beauty and romantic mountain backdrop; Rannoch Moor, one of the last great wildernesses in Britain; and Glen Coe, stark and austere as befits its murderous history.

Best of all, however, are the hills. From Ben Lomond to Ben Nevis, the Highland High Way is packed full of classic mountain walks. You will relish the wide open spaces of Ben Lui and Ben Oss, the dramatic curves of Beinn Dorain and the nail-biting narrowness of the Aonach Eagach, perched high above Glen Coe. You will stride across Black Mount, one of the classic hill-walks with its spectacular ridges and corries, not to mention stunning views across Rannoch Moor. You will enjoy a Munro-bagging extravaganza in the Mamores, surely one of the finest mountain ranges in Britain. The final triumph is an exhilarating ascent of Ben Nevis along the Carn Mor Dearg arête.

The Highland High Way passes through areas rich in plant- and birdlife and places steeped in Scottish history. In this wild country noble stags watch over their herds, golden eagles soar above the hills in search of prey, and the fox leaves its tell-tale footprints in the snow. In these hills clan legend was created by heroes such as Rob Roy MacGregor and villains like the Campbell clan, perpetrators of the brutal massacre of Glen Coe. The beautiful colours and sweeping grandeur of these hills has inspired Robert Louis Stevenson and Sir Walter Scott, William Wordsworth and Robert Burns.

The Highland High Way offers you a route through this splendid scenery across the hills and glens. To make sure you enjoy it to the full, the book includes highlights of the history, geography and wildlife which have shaped the land you see today.

HOW TO USE THIS BOOK

The Highland High Way is not an official long-distance route. There are no waymarkers or signs along it. It makes use of tracks and stalkers' paths where these exist, but there are sections which cross open countryside, with nothing to guide you but your own navigation and map-reading skills.

It is a challenging route but one which is well within the capabilities of any fit and experienced hill walker. It is broken up into one-day sections with a choice of accommodation each night. The challenges build as the route develops. From the relatively gentle territory of the southern Highlands, the route gradually becomes more rugged as it heads north. Walking always gives plenty of time to appreciate the changing scenery; walking the Highland High

Way will give you the extra satisfaction of completing a memorable trek through Scotland's finest hills.

This book gives all the information needed to prepare for and undertake the journey. Each chapter includes a sketch map and detailed description of the route. You should use these, in conjunction with the relevant Ordnance Survey maps, to build up a detailed route plan for each day. The sketch maps are only an aid to route-planning and are not sufficiently detailed to complete the route in safety.

The length of each day's walk and an estimated journey time are also given. The times must be treated as approximate. They assume walkers are reasonably fit and not over-burdened with heavy equipment, and that walking conditions are reasonable. Rain, snow and poor visibility will increase the journey times substantially. Use the times as a rough guide initially; after walking the early sections you will be able to assess how your progress compares with the times given. Naismith's rule is a useful guide for estimating your own route times. It suggests that the average walking speed is three miles an hour, plus an extra half hour for each 300m of ascent. Again, bad weather and heavy rucksacks will increase these averages substantially. Allow extra time on each day's journey for rest breaks, photo stops and just to admire the glorious mountain scenery.

Some suggestions for accommodation and other services on the route are given at the end of each section. Accommodation availability changes rapidly and you should consult local tourist information offices to check details before setting out. Telephone numbers for the offices on the route are also given.

Heading north

Scottish Natural Heritage produce a leaflet on the West Highland Way which lists accommodation and services along the route. It is updated annually and may also be useful for those walking the Highland High Way. The address is given at the back of the book.

One of the attractions of the route described in this book is the range of services you will come across on the way. You can camp, stay in budget accommodation such as youth hostels and bunk-houses, or in bed & breakfasts and hotels virtually every night. Obviously, all accommodation is of limited availability and you would have to travel some distance to find an alternative place to stay if your first choice is full up. It is advisable to book in advance, particularly if you are walking in the busy summer months.

For much of its length, the Highland High Way is close to the West Highland Way, the official long-distance path between Glasgow and Fort William. While the Highland High Way heads over hills and through deserted glens, the West Highland Way takes a low-level route along drove roads and old military routes, waymarked with thistles on wooden posts. The two routes can easily be combined, so that you can alternate flat walking with days in the hills. It is also a good way for groups of walkers of different levels of experience and ability to walk the different routes during the day and meet up in the evening.

The route does not have to be completed in one go. Details of transport to and from each section of the route are included for those who want to do only parts of it. Bear in mind that shops, banks and other services are limited on the route, so plan for this accordingly.

Walking the route from Drymen to Fort William takes eight days. Four extra excursions are suggested which could enable you to extend the route to a two-week holiday. The excursions include bagging four Munros in the Mamores, an ascent of Scotland's most photographed hill, the Buachaille Etive Mor in Glen Coe, and a high moorland walk at the top of Loch Lomond. Topping it all, an ascent of Ben Nevis, via the Carn Mor Dearg arête. The added attraction of these excursions is that you can enjoy walking with just a day-pack, rather than a full rucksack.

The route is particularly good for dedicated Munro-baggers. Munros are Scottish peaks of 3,000 feet (914m) and over, as compiled by Sir Hugh T. Munro in 1891. He listed 283 of them, together with a further 255 'tops' which did not qualify as separate mountains. Subsequent revisions have cut that to 277 Munros and 240 tops, although some purists still stick to Sir Hugh's original classification. In the last 20 years, Munro-bagging has developed into one of Scotland's national sports. More and more people are setting themselves the target of reaching the top of all 277, and a growing number have completed them more than once. A few have ticked them all off in one winter season and others have tackled them on skis or – although this is not recommended – on mountain-bikes.

The eight-day route takes in 14 Munros and the four excursions bring the tally to an impressive 23. It starts with the most southerly, Ben Lomond, and ends with the highest, Ben Nevis. Newcomers to Munro-bagging will still have some way to go, but completing the Highland High Way makes an impressive start and is guaranteed to get you hooked on the sport.

Another attraction of the route is that it includes some unusual approaches to the hills. Heading to the hills for day-trips usually means going up and down the hill by the same path. The Highland High Way never does that, even on the excursions. Each day is a progression through the hills, leading from one stopping-place to another.

Every effort has been made to ensure this book is accurate and comprehensive. No responsibility can be accepted for any errors or omissions, but the authors would be glad to hear if you come across any so that subsequent editions can be updated.

The Highland High Way is one of the finest walks in Scotland. To enjoy it to the full, set out properly prepared and suitably equipped. The next chapter includes useful guidance to make sure you get the most out of your walking and come back safely from the hills.

Mountain Essentials

The Highland High Way passes through some of Scotland's most beautiful scenery. The route, wild and remote in parts, goes across open countryside where you will be some distance from the nearest road, let alone any help. The weather is unpredictable and can change from brilliant sunshine to driving rain or snow in a matter of minutes.

That said, the route is well within the capabilities of anyone with experience of hill-walking. Experience is, however, the key word: anyone setting off must be suitably equipped, confident of their skills on the hill and of their ability to cope with the unexpected.

This chapter will help you prepare so that you get the best out of the Highland High Way. It includes sections on equipment and clothing, navigation, dealing with emergencies and the law in Scotland as it affects hill-walking. Much of it is common sense, and will be familiar to anyone who has spent any time in the hills. It is, however, worth repeating. If you set out properly prepared, you are more likely to return safe and satisfied, having enjoyed the achievement of completing the route.

FOLLOWING THE ROUTE

The Highland High Way is not a waymarked route. It goes across high mountains, sometimes on paths and sometimes across open countryside. In all, it requires some 11,000m of ascent – more than the height of Everest. The time spent walking is not short – an average of eight hours and 14 miles each day. Much of the walking is straightforward and, in the northern stretches, on well-trodden paths. But some sections are more difficult and strenuous, with no paths to help route-finding.

The route climbs above 900m on all but the first day and, on some days, there are several peaks above this height. Sections of the route involve scrambling up steep, rocky slopes. Others require you to navigate your way across featureless moorland. The Aonach Eagach, which you will cross on the seventh day, is the narrowest and most challenging ridge-walk on the British mainland.

You will be better able to cope with these challenges if you build up your fitness before you begin the route. That will make the first days, when you will be crossing rough terrain and getting used to your pack, more enjoyable. The route does break you in gently, with the hills getting higher and more rugged the further along the route you go. The weather in the southern stretches is also likely to be less severe than at the higher altitudes as you progress along the route. Even the first day, where the maximum height is only 596m, is challenging enough. Be sure that everyone in the party can cope with the demands of the route.

ROUTE CARD

Date

Objective

From

To

Magnetic bearing

Distance

Ground

Time

Total time

Plus ten minutes per hour

Start time

End time

Escape routes

| 1 | 2 | 3 | 4 |

NAVIGATION

Each section includes a map and a brief summary of the day's walk and detailed instructions for following the route. These maps are designed to help you plan the route but they are not enough on their own. They must be used in conjunction with Ordnance Survey maps. The maps covering the Highland High Way are the Ordnance Survey Landranger series:

57 Stirling and the Trossachs
56 Loch Lomond and Inveraray
50 Glen Orchy
41 Ben Nevis and Fort William

You should plan each day's walk in advance using the OS maps and directions given in each section. Be prepared to vary the route or to cut it short, depending on weather conditions and the fitness of those in the party. Suggestions on how to shorten the route are given for each section; these should be studied as an essential part of the preparation for the day's walk. A route plan outlining the day's walk, key points of navigation and possible variations, is a valuable tool. A sample is shown opposite.

You must have a compass and know how to use it. An easy walk in good weather, when paths, hills and other landmarks are clear, can become treacherous in poor visibility. Mist and low cloud can shroud the mountains at any time – the summit of Ben Nevis, for example, is clear only 60 days a year on average. It is all too easy to stray from the route in poor visibility. Not only could that take you far from your destination, it could also lead you into dangerous terrain. Even the gentlest hills on the Highland High Way have cliffs, crags and gullies which can trap those lost in mist. Waiting until the mist clears should only be contemplated as a last resort; it can take hours or even days to lift. In the meantime, you will become increasingly tired, cold and miserable and run the risk of exposure.

It is essential that you are able to set a compass bearing, and have the confidence to stick to it. It is not difficult; the instructions provided with most suitable compasses give a useful introduction to direction-finding skills. Practising in familiar territory and good weather will develop your confidence, something which could be invaluable when you have to set a course in more difficult conditions.

WHEN TO GO

The route can be tackled at any time of the year and every season has its attractions. Winter can be the most beautiful time in the Highlands. The hills are at their most majestic when covered with snow and framed by a clear blue sky. In spring the tops are still likely to have some snow but the lower slopes are dotted with the delicate purples, yellows and blues of saxifrage, campion and harebell, and in the later months you'll find rhododendrons and azaleas. In summer the days are long and the climate at its most gentle. In the autumn the purple glow of the heather and the gold blaze of bracken makes the braes alive with vivid colour.

All the seasons have disadvantages, too. Winter days are short and conditions arduous. In spring the burns will be high and the ground can be very wet. Summer is busy and afflicted by midges. In autumn, good weather can deteriorate very quickly.

Deciding when to go, therefore, depends on your own preference and experience. You should not contemplate setting off between November and March unless you are skilled in winter mountaineering, with experience of using ropes, crampons and ice-axes. Snow-covered hills may be beautiful but they are also dangerous. Cornices form on the high ridges and above corries, and can be treacherous unless you know how to cross them safely. Ice can make even the easiest of scrambles a severe test of winter climbing skill. Avalanches are a serious risk in many corries and gullies. Freezing winds and driving snow can produce arctic conditions on the high tops.

Late spring and early summer is a good time to walk the Highland High Way as May and June are usually the driest and sunniest months. In June particularly, the days are long – late in the month it hardly gets dark at all. The light early in the day can be clear and sharp so you can enjoy the splendid views along the route at their best. There are also fewer visitors to Scotland early in the summer, so accommodation is easier to find. July and August are warm but usually wetter than the early summer months. They are also the prime time for midges, the curse of the Scottish summer, which in some areas can make being out of doors very unpleasant. The glorious purples, golds and greens of the autumn hills mean that September and October have a lot to recommend them. September in particular is often blessed with warm, clear days.

WIND CHILL TEMPERATURES IN THE HILLS

The combined effect of falling temperatures and increasing windspeed on the apparent temperature

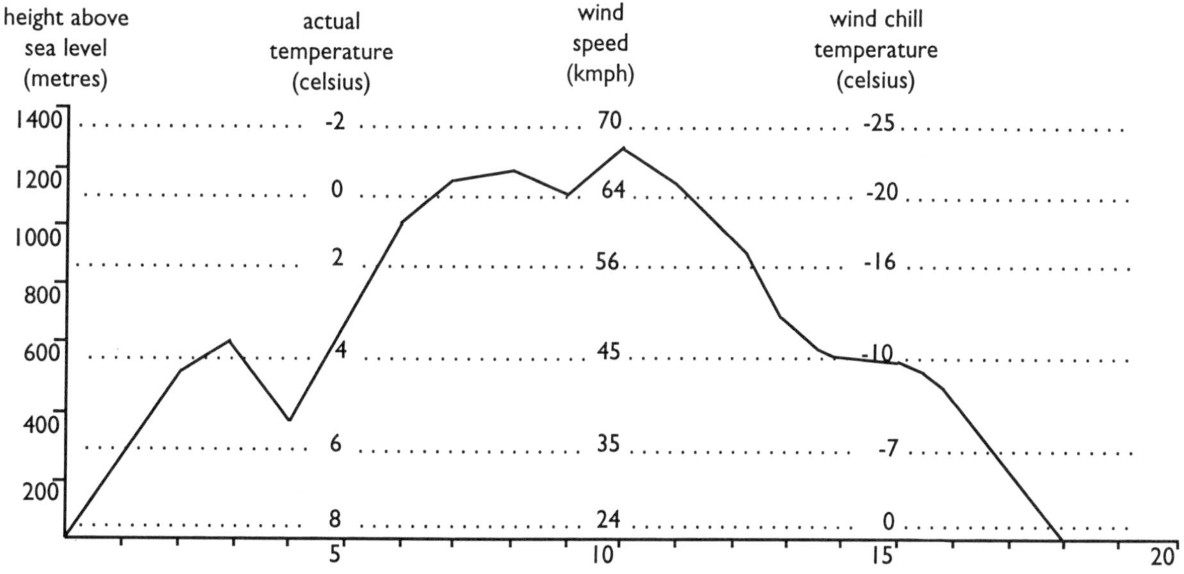

height above sea level (metres)

actual temperature (celsius)

wind speed (kmph)

wind chill temperature (celsius)

height above sea level (metres)	actual temperature (celsius)	wind speed (kmph)	wind chill temperature (celsius)
1400	-2	70	-25
1200	0	64	-20
1000	2	56	-16
800			
600	4	45	-10
400	6	35	-7
200	8	24	0
	5	10	15	20

This book describes the route going from south to north. You can, of course, go in the opposite direction but it is not recommended. The further north you go, the more rugged the terrain becomes. Walking the southern sections first will prepare you for the more rugged hills to come. The prevailing winds will be behind you, rather than in front, if you start at Drymen. Starting at Fort William and heading south means both these advantages are lost.

WEATHER

On a clear day it is possible to see the final Munro of the route, Ben Nevis, from the summit of the first, Ben Lomond. Such days are rare, though. The weather cannot be taken for granted in any season. The hills on the route are the first obstacles to weather fronts as they blow in from the Atlantic on the prevailing westerly winds. That means conditions can change rapidly. The most frequent hazard is mist and low cloud which can descend suddenly at any time of the year. This can be very disorientating. If mist threatens, fix your position carefully and make frequent use of map and compass to get off the hill safely.

On Ben Nevis snow can fall even in August, and on all the peaks along the Highland High Way there can be snowstorms late into the spring. You can encounter snowfields as late as May or June. Lying snow gives completely different walking conditions. Falling snow can make navigation difficult.

Weather conditions on the hills can be dramatically different to those at low level. Temperatures fall between two and three degrees Celsuis for every 300m of ascent. Wind speeds on the summit or on exposed cols and ridges can be three times those lower down the hill. High winds, combined with falling temperatures, can make it feel very cold on the hills. As the diagram on p.20 illustrates, the effect of wind and temperature can produce radically different conditions on the summit to those in the glen below.

Walking against strong winds is difficult and exhausting. In such conditions, avoid summits and exposed passes and stay in the lea of the hill wherever possible. Roping together in very strong winds can make you feel safer.

Loch Sloy, which lies below Ben Vorlich on Day 3 of the route, holds the record for the highest rainfall in 24 hours on the British mainland, but many other parts of the route run it a close second. Scotland can be very wet indeed and, like wind, rain increases with altitude – Ben Nevis, for example, gets double the rainfall of Fort William.

Rain makes the terrain more treacherous. Bogs will be wetter, grass and rocks slippier and burns can turn into raging torrents in a matter of hours after heavy rain. Crossing a burn after a downpour can be difficult and dangerous and should be avoided. If it is not possible to alter the route to avoid crossing a burn, there are various ways to make it safer. Crossing in a line, each facing upstream with the strongest person at the front and using a pole for support, is one option. Another is to cross in a huddle, arms around each other's shoulders. The safest place to cross is where the river runs in a straight line, or widens, but not at a bend.

Scotland does have its fair share of sunshine and that too can be a hazard to walkers. A breeze and the cooler air at altitude can make you forget the power of the sun's rays, but sunburn, sunstroke and dehydration are real dangers on sunny days. To avoid the unpleasant effects of too much sun, protect your head and neck with a hat or a scarf, drink plenty of water and use sunscreen on all exposed parts of the body.

You must have an accurate weather forecast before setting out each day. National forecasts are usually too general to be useful; the shipping forecast for Mallin, the sea area nearest the Highland High Way, on the other hand, gives better guidance on the wind and rain conditions likely on the hills. Local television and radio forecasts are more detailed than national ones and often include specific reports on mountain weather. Specialist telephone services, like Mountaincall or Weathercall, cover smaller areas and have the advantage of being available by telephone wherever you are on the route. The number for Mountaincall, which gives conditions on the hills, is 0898 500 441. Weathercall, which gives a five-day forecast, is 0898 500 421.

CLOTHING

The more comfortable your clothing, the more you will enjoy the Highland High Way. Strong, comfortable footwear is the most essential requirement. Boots should be sturdy enough to support your feet and ankles on the rugged terrain you will pass through. If you are walking in winter, they should also be rigid enough to take crampons. They should be well worn-in to ensure they are comfortable enough to sustain you through the long days in the hills.

Completely waterproof boots are, perhaps, an impossible dream but footwear should be designed to keep out rain and as much of the water from bogs and streams as possible. The most waterproof are those with no lace-holes, a sewn-in tongue and no seams. Maintain your boots by applying water-proofing regularly. Socks should be thick and have no seams to chafe the heels and toes. Gaiters will help keep socks and trousers drier and cleaner when the weather is wet or wintry.

Attend to blisters and other problems immedi-ately. The longer you ignore rubbing, the worse the blister will become and the more uncomfortable it will be to walk. Plasters or tape and lint padding are fine for most injuries, and more modern 'second skin' treatments are also effective. Giving feet an airing by removing socks and boots in the middle of the day, if the weather is good, is refreshing and can help to prevent blisters.

It may be a cliché but it is nonetheless true that you can encounter four seasons in one day on the Scottish hills. You must be prepared for all of them. The best way is to have plenty of layers of clothing. A number of thin layers is a more effective way of keeping warm than one thick one, and easier to shed when the effort of climbing warms you up. Wind can quickly chill you, so it is important that at least one of your layers is windproof. Start with a T-shirt or something similar, and add a shirt and a fleece jacket, sweatshirt or other tops as necessary. A good waterproof layer is essential. Breathable jackets and trousers made from fabric such as Gore-Tex may be more expensive than plastic-coated nylon but they are more comfortable if you have to wear them all day. Jeans are not suitable for walking. They chafe, are heavier than cotton trousers, leggings or cords, and are very difficult to dry out if they get wet. Waterproof trousers to wear over the top are essential and must be easy to get on and off.

Your hands and head can get cold quickly. Carry gloves and a woolly hat, whatever the season, as the tops of hills can be cold at any time of year. In winter and spring a balaclava will protect the neck and face from driving snow and rain.

EQUIPMENT

The equipment you need depends on the time of year and which type of accommodation you choose. It is possible to stay in hotels or bed & breakfasts every night, so in the summer months you may need only a few changes of clothing, essential wet-weather gear and basic toiletries in your rucksack. If you decide to stay in hostels and bunkhouses, you will have to add a towel and sleeping-bag to the basic list. If you are camping, on the other hand, tents, food and cooking equipment will have to be carried. Spending a few weekends preparing yourself for the extra demands of the route, and for checking equipment, is useful if you are not accustomed to carrying a heavy pack. The key is to keep weight to a minimum. Some parts of the walk are steep and rocky, so the more you are carrying, the harder and slower the going, and the greater the risk of accident or injury.

The rucksack must keep clothes dry and clean. No rucksack is completely waterproof, so you should use a strong polythene rucksack liner. Ideally, the rucksack straps should be adjustable, and should be balanced to spread the weight across your shoulders, back and hips.

Most people return safely from the hills without encountering any problems. Unless you are unlucky, you will too, but it is best to be prepared for the worst. Everyone in the party should carry a survival bag in case bad weather, injury or unexpected delays mean you cannot get off the hill safely before dark. Survival bags provide insulation and act as a break against wind and rain. The sturdier the bag, the better; space-age foil ones tear easily and are difficult to handle in the wind and rain.

Take a torch and spare batteries, both to see in the dark and to signal for help in an emergency. Six flashes, repeated at intervals of one minute, is the recognised mountain distress signal. Carry a whistle too in case you need to call for help – six blasts, a minute's silence and a further six blasts is the emergency signal.

A first-aid kit containing plasters, bandages, lint, antiseptic wash, painkillers, glucose tablets and antiseptic cream should be easily accessible in the rucksack. The kit should also include insect repellent, anti-histamine cream and sun cream.

Dehydration is a risk on the hills. It increases tiredness and forces the body to work harder to supply vital nutrients to the muscles. Unless you replace the lost liquid, you will get tired quickly. You should carry a sturdy one-litre water bottle and take frequent drinks from it. In summer you may need to carry more than one bottle as the springs and burns higher up the hills can run dry. A knife and some spare high-energy emergency food, like Kendal mint cake, chocolate or dried fruit, complete the basic requirements.

If you are walking the route in winter, you will need an ice-axe, crampons and a rope – and experience in using them. In fact, a length of rope is a useful addition to your kit at any time of the year. The Scottish Mountaineering Council guide suggests inexperienced walkers use a rope on sections of the Aonach Eagach.

Although accommodation is available every night, shops, banks and other services are few and far between. There is no shop between Drymen, the starting point, and Tyndrum, reached at the end of Day 4, except for a small store at Beinglas farm. After Tyndrum, the next shop is in Kinlochleven on the penultimate day of the route. There is no bank between Drymen and Kinlochleven. You should therefore plan ahead and ensure you have sufficient supplies and funds to complete the route.

SAFETY ON THE HILLS

No matter how well planned the day's walk, accidents can happen. They will be far less threatening if you are prepared to deal with them. The most important preparation is to make sure someone knows where you are. If you are booking accommodation in advance, let the hotel or hostel know when you expect to arrive and which route you will take to get there. Phone them if your plans change and you will save a lot of unnecessary concern. If you are camping, or hoping to find accommodation as you go, tell someone where you are going before you set off in the morning and arrange to telephone them when you arrive in the evening. Remember to let people know you have arrived at your destination. It is frustrating for the rescue services to be called out to save someone who has not bothered to report that they are safely off the hills.

Many people walk on their own and come to no harm; unless you are very capable and experienced, though, you should always go with at least one other person, who can go for help should it be needed. If there is an accident, try not to panic. Slow down and think things through thoroughly; don't just choose the first or easiest option as this could make the situation worse. Don't be tempted to take a quicker but riskier route off the mountain because the weather is deteriorating or because someone needs help. As well as increasing the risk of further accidents, this could make it harder for the rescue services to find you if they are called out.

First-aid knowledge and the ability to assess the seriousness of an injury can be invaluable. When an accident has occurred, someone should stay with the injured person if possible to ensure that he or she is kept warm and comfortable. When going for help, know the exact location of those still on the hill so that the rescue services can pinpoint them accurately. Using a rescue message form to record details of location, injuries and so on will help to focus the mind. Ensure, too, that the person going for help knows how to get off the hill and is fit and experienced enough to do so. Another accident on the descent will hardly help the situation.

If you have to stay on the mountain overnight because of delay or bad weather, or because a member of the party is unable to cope with the descent, the following guidelines will help you prepare an emergency bivouac:

(1) Shelter from the wind behind rocks or by moving downhill if possible. In snow, dig a simple cave or hollow to climb into.

(2) Wear any spare clothing but remove tight-fitting garments, boot-laces etc.

(3) Insulate yourself from the cold ground by lying on rucksacks, carry mats and so on.

(4) Get inside survival bags quickly; sharing one between two will help to retain body heat.

(5) Share small quantities of food and drink throughout the night.

(6) Look after each other and watch for signs of deterioration in your companions.

(7) Be aware of the signs of mountain hypothermia. These include tiredness, cramps, lethargy and slurred speech.

An excellent guide to survival on the hills, *Safety on Mountains*, is available from the British Mountaineering Council. Their address is in the section on suggested further reading at the back of the book.

THE MOUNTAIN CODE

The tradition in Scotland is that everyone has the right to roam unchallenged in the hills. This, however, is tradition not law. There are few public rights-of-way; elsewhere, access to the hills depends on the consent of the landowner. Please note that the inclusion of a particular route in this book does not imply that it is a right-of-way.

In practice, access to the hills is rarely refused to considerate walkers. Many landowners will ask you to keep to particular routes or paths, or to avoid certain hills during the deerstalking season (July to October) and during the grouse-shooting season (12 August to 10 December). Anyone on the Highland High Way during these months should contact the local estate office to check on restrictions. Addresses and telephone numbers for each section of the route are given at the end of the respective chapters. *Heading for the Scottish Hills*, published by the Scottish Mountaineering Trust, gives useful advice on access to the hills as well as details of estates' ownership.

Walkers should also be careful not to disturb sheep in the lambing season between April and May. An alternative route is given for the first stage of the route, between Drymen and Rowardennan, which must be used when lambing is in progress.

Landowners are more likely to remain well disposed to walkers if they are courteous and considerate. It is important to follow the mountain code – it makes the hills more pleasant for all walkers and safeguards them for future generations. The points of the code are:

(1) Guard against the risk of fire.
(2) Fasten all gates. Use gates and stiles where possible. If it is necessary to climb a fence or wall, take care not to damage it.
(3) Keep dogs under control.
(4) Keep to paths where they exist. Circling round boggy sections, or taking a short-cut on zigzags, extends the area of erosion.
(5) Leave no litter.
(6) Safeguard water supplies. Do not pollute burns and streams, toilet well away from them.
(7) Protect wildlife, plants and trees.
(8) Go carefully on country roads.
(9) Respect the life and work of the countryside.

The Highland High Way is an enjoyable and challenging walk through spectacular countryside. Observing these simple guidelines will make sure you enjoy it to the full. Proper preparation for the route and respect for the conditions that you could meet in the mountains will enable you to complete the route in safety and to recall the adventure with pride.

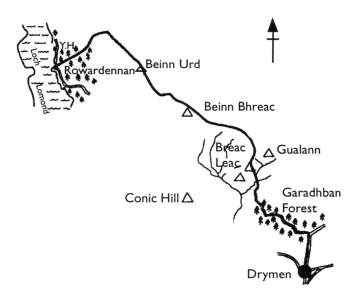

Day 1

Drymen to Rowardennan

Day 1
The Road to the Highlands

Drymen to Rowardennan

ROUTE SUMMARY
From the Square in Drymen take the road north to the Garadhban forest. Follow the West Highland Way markers through the forest then go north over the hill between Breac Leac and Gualann to where the Loch Ard forest rises to the ridge. Continue north-west over Beinn Bhreac and Beinn Uird and join the Ben Lomond tourist path to descend to Rowardennan.

Distance: 21km
Time: 7hr 15min
Ascent: 813m
Descent: 853m

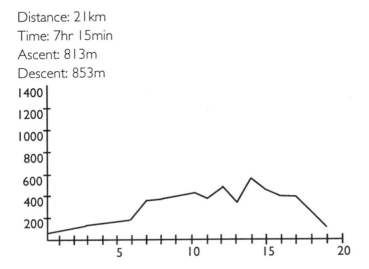

The Highland High Way starts at Drymen, a typical lowland village with pretty white buildings grouped around a green. The landcape quickly becomes more rugged, however. At first, the scenery is dominated by the gentle braes of the Campsie Fells and the Fintry hills to the south and east. These are soon joined by views of the Luss hills across Loch Lomond in the west. While their slopes are still green and rolling, already they rise 200m or more above the lowland hills you are leaving behind. The deeply cleft glens and passes which run between the Luss hills hint at the grandeur which lies ahead.

As you head further north, the majesty of Scotland's finest scenery begins to unfold. First come the Arrochar Alps, with The Cobbler's famous triple-cragged peak standing proud in the north-west. Next Ben Lomond, the first Munro on the Highland High Way, rises in splendid isolation on the east side of Loch Lomond. The loch itself, one of the most beautiful in the country, is a perfect backdrop to the rugged hills.

Today is intended to ease you into the demands of eight days' walking in the high hills. It will get your feet accustomed to your boots, your legs adjusted to the terrain and your pack settled comfortably on your back. There are no big hills – the highest point, the summit of Beinn Uird, is just 596m – and the terrain is relatively gentle. At around seven hours' walking, given reasonable weather conditions, today is also one of the shortest days on the Highland High Way.

It is not a day to be underestimated, though. Some of the walking is over peat and heather moorland, which remains wet in even the driest of summers.

The slopes on one section are riven with drainage ditches, so you have to be careful where you put your feet. You need good navigation skills here, as much as on the higher peaks further north, particularly in poor visibility.

This is not only a day of preparation for the physical challenges ahead; it is also the start of a major expedition in other ways too. Drymen is the last village until you reach Tyndrum, four days' walk away – five if you plan to include the An Caisteal excursion from Inverarnan. Most of the hotels and guest-houses on the route provide packed lunches, and most bars have meals in the evening, but there are few other places to buy food and supplies. If you intend to be self-sufficient, it is sensible to stock up at the store in the village. Drymen also offers the last bank until Kinlochleven – and there, the bank is only open on Thursdays.

The route starts at the side of the Clachan Inn in a corner of the square. A plaque by the door boasts that the inn was founded in 1734 making it, so it claims, the oldest in Scotland. More relevant for walkers is the good bar food it offers if you stay in one of the many bed & breakfasts or the campsite in Drymen before starting out.

Follow Main Street north by the side of the pub past a health centre and a sports centre before heading out into open farmland. Views of the route ahead quickly begin to open out, with Conic Hill coming into view on the left just after you pass the sports centre. After about 20 minutes, the road turns sharply right. Leave the road here and go through the metal gate which leads to a forest track.

Follow the track west until you reach a junction, where you turn right. A short distance further along, the track meets the West Highland Way. Turn left and follow the waymarkers through the forest. This is one of the few times the Highland High Way meets the low-level route. (The next long section is not until after Tyndrum on the way to climb Beinn Dorain). Having joined the West Highland Way, the route continues north-west through the Garadhban forest, part of the much larger Queen Elizabeth Forest Park which stretches for 50,000 acres north as far as Loch Katrine. The spruce and douglas firs mark it out as a commercially planted forest, but the larch and birch interspersed with the conifers makes it less dreary to walk through than many plantations. Clearings made by logging and winter storms give some views aross the surrounding countryside, although these will be reduced as the replanting matures. The views disappear as you progress into the forest and the track narrows to a path.

In the lambing season in April and May, the West Highland Way is diverted away from Conic Hill to avoid disturbing the sheep. Walkers are instead sent along the road to Balmaha, through Milton of Buchanan. That diversion also applies to the Highland High Way during lambing and means following the West Highland Way along the banks of Loch Lomond to Rowardennan. Advice on when the route is closed is available from the Tourist Information office in Balmaha.

A clearing in the trees gives the first views of the southern end of Loch Lomond. Shortly after this, where the path narrows, the Forestry Commission has provided a rough camping area to the right of the path. This is an alternative to the campsite in Drymen, but in summer the midges are even more of a plague here than in the open. In more exposed campsites, there is always a chance of a breeze to keep the midges down

The path leaves the forest across a stile which, although it looks high now, has been reduced in height as the forest has matured and needs less protection from the deer. It was once the highest stile in Scotland. Cross it and carry on along the waymarked West Highland Way until it veers sharply west towards Conic Hill. Instead of following it, the Highland High Way keeps east of Conic Hill and heads north towards the southern slopes of Ben Lomond.

Sheep-farming is important in this area and dogs are not permitted. Anyone with a dog must follow the road into Balmaha, signposted in the Garadhban forest.

This high-level route was the one originally proposed for the official West Highland Way but,

Ben Lomond

after consultation with local landowners, it was decided to go through Balmaha and along the banks of Loch Lomond instead.

Looking west from here, a line of islands lead like stepping-stones across Loch Lomond to the cleft of Glen Luss, visible on the western bank of the loch. This is the Highland Boundary Fault, which runs from Bute in the south-west of Scotland to Stonehaven in the north-east, and which crosses Loch Lomond and Conic Hill at this point. The tensions which caused the fault date back millions of years, but there are still occasional movements today. A distinct change in the terrain clearly identifies the geological transformations taking place below the earth's surface as you cross from the Lowlands to the Highlands. To the south, easily eroded red sandstone rock gives the rolling braes and gentle glens characteristic of southern Scotland. The more resistant schists, quartzites and granites to the north of the Highland Boundary Fault are among the oldest in the world. Their hardness, and the impact of the ice sheets which scarred them, is evident in the rocky peaks, sheer cliffs and sharp ridges which are a feature of the hills north of the Fault. The impervious rocks in the north also give rise to one of the less pleasant aspects of the Scottish landscape – peat bogs. There are few places for water to drain through the solid granite and quartzite rocks. Instead, it lies in the humus layer above the base rocks, creating bogs and sodden ground wherever the land is too flat to allow the rain to drain away easily.

Where the West Highland Way turns left towards Conic Hill, head through a metal gate in the wall to the open moorland beyond. Continue northwards towards the unnamed middle summit between Breac Leac and Gualann, which lie east of Conic Hill. The ground is wettest on the floor of the glen. Aiming for the higher ground in the east before turning north up the hill will avoid the worst of the bog and make the going easier.

The route now goes across trackless, rough ground until you reach the ridge of Beinn Breac. Hidden burns and drainage channels can make the going arduous, particularly in wet weather. Care is needed to avoid an ankle-wrenching stumble into one of these ditches. Use the sheep tracks which criss-cross the glen to skirt east and then north-east to the unnamed summit. The going improves after you cross the Kilandan burn, and the climb up the south side of the hill is drier and easier underfoot.

From the summit of the unnamed hill, which hardly seems high enough to deserve its distinction as the first ascent on the Highland High Way, head north-east towards the mature trees on the horizon which mark the western edge of the Loch Ard Forest. This is another section of the Queen Elizabeth Forest Park. Take care on the first part of the descent, where the slope is steep and grassy.

As you cross north-east towards the forest from the first summit, you will pass a line of abandoned fence posts. Follow these north until they meet a high deer fence which surrounds the forest. Follow the deer fence until it veers north, then carry on north-west, heading for the rocky outcrop on the ridge line ahead of you. This marks the start of the ridge which heads north-west to the summit of Stob a' Choin Duibh and on to Beinn Bhreac.

The climb to the rocky tor at the start of the ridge gives good views south to the Campsie Fells and towards Loch Lomond and some of its islands in the west. There are 38 islands in Loch Lomond, all of which were inhabited at one time or another. They were used as places of worship, as clan strongholds and as refuges away from the plagues which swept the mainland in the Middle Ages. Some were used as a place to distil illicit whisky in shebeens, others for alcoholics to dry out.

The largest and most southerly of the islands is Inchmurrin, which guards the entrance to the bay on Loch Lomond's southern tip. Named after Saint Mirrin, who established an early Christian church there, the Statistical Account of 1773 records the island's infamous past: 'Many persons disordered in their senses were sent to it as a place of confinement.' 'Disordered' was clearly rather a loose term. It included 'those of the fair sex, who were unfortunate as to give pregnant proof of their frailty' who were sent here to avoid the 'reproof of the world'. Not only did these women have to contend with being classified insane for being pregnant while unmarried, the Account also records that they had to suffer the attentions of a woodcutter, who provided lodgings for some of the women on the island, plus the additional burden of falling within the parish of a clergyman who was 'a zealous campaigner against fornicators'. The island was later used by the Duke of Montrose as a deer park, while a now-ruined castle on it was once home to the earls of Lennox.

The second-largest island, Inchlonaig, 'island of the marshes', lies directly south-west of this viewpoint. It has a forest of yew trees planted by

Robert the Bruce to ensure there was a constant supply of wood to make bows for his archers. Another, Inchcailloch, 'the island of women', which is the first of the island-steps across the loch from Conic Hill, is named after a nunnery that was established there.

The islands, together with the lack of development on the east side of the loch, mean Loch Lomond is rich with birdlife. The central section of its eastern bank is a nature reserve and bird sanctuary, Loch Lomond Park. Two hundred species of birds and more than a quarter of all the wild plants present in Britain have been spotted here. Birdlife ranges from birds of prey, including golden eagles and buzzards, to smaller migrants like redstarts and pied flycatchers. In autumn and winter the loch is home to waders and geese, particularly Greenland white fronts. Herds of deer are often seen, particularly in the winter. Here, they are generally

Loch Lomond from Rowardennan

41

the smaller fallow and roe deer. Further north their larger cousins, red deer, are more frequent.

Continue north-west and the deer fence rises to meet the ridge again. You will shortly get the first sight of Ben Lomond. The distinctive shape of its steep shoulder rising to a tent-shaped summit dispels any confusion between it and the Arrochar Alps in the west, which are already in view.

Keeping near the fence again gives the best route north-west over a series of low summits. A low fence joins it from the south-west. Cross the lower fence where it joins the deer fence and continue north-west towards the summit of Stob a' Choin Duibh. From there the trig point of Beinn Bhreac can be seen across the low ridge which links the two hills. Descend north-west from Stob a' Choin Duibh then climb again to the neglected trig point of Beinn Bhreac.

From here the hills to the north rise rank upon rank as far as the eye can see. In the north-east are the Crianlarich hills, including the distinctive peaks of Ben More and Stob Binnein, as well as the Trossachs hills further south. To the west are the Arrochar Alps with the distinctive crags of Ben Arthur, The Cobbler, becoming clearer. Straight ahead is Ben Lomond, the first Munro of the Highland High Way.

On the west side of the loch, just south of the Arrochar Alps, lies another Beinn Bhreac which forms one side of Glen Douglas. The variegated colours of heather, grasses and bracken explains the translation, 'speckled hill'. From the eastern Beinn Bhreac the next top, Beinn Uird, is visible in the north-west. A rounded hill, with no obvious summit, it looks lower than Beinn Bhreac, but this is an illusion. You will appreciate that it is higher as you descend to the wide flat area between the two summits and begin to climb Beinn Uird.

Descend north-west from Beinn Bhreac, heading between the two cairned summits to a small lochan visible at the low point of the featureless ridge. That will keep you on the highest ground until you reach the lochan. From there, climb north-west up the wide slopes of Beinn Uird.

Cross the featureless summit plateau and descend the north-west shoulder, heading toward the Glashlet burn which tumbles down through a wide corrie to the right of Ben Lomond's tourist path. After 15 minutes' descent, an indistinct vehicle track descends south-west towards Loch Lomond beginning close to the point marked Elrig on the OS map. Follow this wide but faint track until it meets a clearer track, marked on the OS map, which comes up from Blairvockie. Follow this clear track north-west to where it ends at a series of sheep pens. Pass through the sheep pens and turn right immediately to join the tourist track which climbs Ben Lomond from Rowardennan.

When you reach the tourist track, head downhill. Thirty minutes' walking over sometimes steep rocky slopes, brings you down to the carpark on the lochside. Turn right at the carpark for the youth hostel, left for the Rowardennan Hotel. Camping is available about two miles south down the official West Highland Way by Cashel farm. There is also a bivouac site on the lochside just north of the youth hostel.

USEFUL INFORMATION

Drymen

Accommodation: Buchanan Arms Hotel,
01360 660588
Winnock Hotel, 01360 660245
Mrs Betty Robb, Ceardach, Gartness Road,
01360 660596
Lander Bed & Breakfast, 17 Stirling Road,
01360 660273

Camping: Easter Drumquhassle farm, Gartness
Road, 01360 660893
(also offers bed & breakfast and has wooden
wigwams)

Transport: Buses from Glasgow and Balloch –
Midland Bluebird, 01324 613777

Supplies: Food store and post office in Drymen

Bank: Royal Bank of Scotland, Drymen, open
daily

Stalking/sheep: Mr John Maxwell, Cashel farm,
01360 870229

Tourist Information: Balloch, 01389 753533
Drymen (from May to September), 01360 660068

Rowardennan

Accommodation: Rowardennan Hotel,
01360 870273

Youth hostel: Rowardennan Youth Hostel,
01360 870259

Camping: Two miles south on lochside by Cashel
farm
Bivouac camping just north of youth hostel

Transport: Ferry from Inverbeg, April-September
  Loch Lomond Ferry Services, 01360 870273
Supplies: None
Stalking: National Trust for Scotland. No
  restrictions

Inveruglas

Inversnaid

Loch Arklet

Maol a' Chapuill

Cruachan

Cruinn a'
Bheinn

Loch

Ben Lomond

Ptarmigan

Lomond

Rowardennan

Day 2

Rowardennan to
Inversnaid

Day 2
Ben Lomond

Rowardennan to Inversnaid

ROUTE SUMMARY

From the youth hostel climb the path north up Ptarmigan and then follow the ridge east to Ben Lomond. Go north over Cruinn a' Bheinn and across Gleann Gaoithe to the col between Cruachan and Maol a' Chapuill. Descend north-west, gradually rounding Cruachan, to the road from Aberfoyle to Inversnaid.

Distance: 14km
Time: 6hr 30min
Ascent: 1,307m
Descent: 1,307m

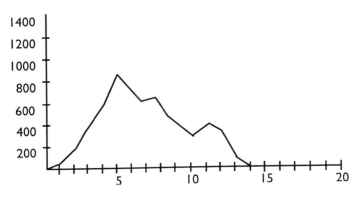

This is a truly glorious day: the walking is not difficult and the views all along the route are superb. The crowning glory is Loch Lomond which here is even more of a feast for the eyes than on yesterday's walk from Drymen. Its beauty grows as the route progresses, its islands glinting like emeralds in the clear water and the greens and browns of the hills forming a perfect frame for its slender curves. The oak woodlands along its bank, once harvested for tannin, vinegar and dye products, soften the steep braes and sharp edges of its shores.

The summit of Ben Lomond is a fine place from which to admire the loch. From there, the contrast between the two ends is clear. In the north it is a narrow, fjord-like strip of water, twisting between steeply rising braes on either side. At its southern end the loch broadens out and the slopes to its banks become much more gentle. The difference between the two ends of the loch is a legacy of the Loch Lomond Advance which created it some 9,000 years ago. Huge glaciers gouged a path through the surrounding hills, cutting a deep, narrow trench in the north, where the hills were made of more resistant rock. Below the Highland faultline, the red sandstone gave more easily against the glacier's force so it spread over a wider area. The contrast is evident underwater too; at the north of the loch, where the glacial action was strongest, it falls to a depth of nearly 200m; in the south, it is only a tenth of that.

Glaciers were also responsible for making it Britain's largest body of freshwater, rather than a continuation of the sea-loch, Loch Long. The retreating glaciers deposited a moraine which formed a plug separating Loch Lomond from Loch Long.

Measuring 23 miles from north to south, Loch Lomond is one of the longest lochs in Scotland. On a more functional note, it keeps much of central Scotland supplied with water. The 450 million litres run off daily to meet the needs of central Scotland households amounts to just 6 millimetres of the loch's 75 square kilometres surface area.

The beauty of the loch is underscored by the majesty of Ben Lomond, which stands proud halfway up its eastern bank. While the other hills which surround the loch are crowded in by neighbouring summits, Ben Lomond rises up isolated and aloof, like a sentinel monitoring all who pass along the shores below. It is one of Scotland's most distinctive hills and its summit cone, perched above a broad steep bank, makes it instantly recognisable from miles around.

Loch Lomond has long been renowned as one of Scotland's most beautiful lochs. As long ago as AD 800, Nennius described it as 'the first wonder of Britain'. Sir Walter Scott, in his classic novel *Rob Roy*, talks of a 'noble loch . . . one of the most surprising, beautiful and sublime spectacles in nature'. The loch and its hill were both immortalised in one of Scotland's best-known songs, 'The Bonnie Banks o' Loch Lomond'. Written by a condemned Jacobite prisoner awaiting execution in Carlisle jail, it is a love song to the loch as much as to his sweetheart, from whom he parted:

In yon shady glen
On the steep sides of Ben Lomond.

His sweetheart, he says, should:

Tak' the high road
And I'll tak' the low road
And I'll be in Scotland afore ye.

The high road refers to the overground route back to Scotland while the low road, which the Jacobite

Loch Lomond and Rowardennan

knows he is condemned to take, is the spiritual route back through the earth. Alas, he laments:

Me and my true love will never meet again,
On the bonnie, bonnie banks o' Loch Lomond.

The beauty of the loch is widely appreciated. On fine summer days it attracts day-trippers from

Glasgow and visitors from much further afield to play on its banks and sail round its islands. Heavy tourist traffic will not spoil the scenery today, though. Most of the tourist trade is confined to the west side of the loch, where the busy A82 gives easy access for cars. Many of those who head for the east side of the loch do so to climb Ben Lomond, one of Scotland's favourite hills, which was described in 1811 as 'an ascent without toil or difficulty; a mere walk of pleasure'. The same holds true today. The Highland High Way avoids the tourist track up the southern ridge. Instead, it goes along the western flank of the hill to the outlying top of Ptarmigan and heads east from there to the summit. This route is quieter than the main tourist path and gives the most attractive views of the loch and its shore. Few choose to descend from Ben Lomond to Inversnaid so you will have the pleasure of walking for most of the day in isolation, disturbed only by the visit to the summit. The hill is owned by the National Trust so there are no restrictions on access.

The ascent starts north of the Rowardennan youth hostel. Take the narrow road north along the loch, ignoring the track which leads up to some private cottages on the right. After five minutes you will cross the second bridge since leaving the youth hostel. Beyond it, a path heads off to the right through the trees. Take this path, which zigzags quite steeply upwards, first through woodland and then on pleasant grass slopes. After 20 minutes' steep climbing, the path turns north and crosses Ben Lomond's western flank towards the domed summit of Ptarmigan. As the hill's name suggests, ptarmigan are common in these hills and you may see or hear them as you walk.

Already the views of the loch and its hills are magnificent and the vistas widens as you climb steadily up to Ptarmigan. The path is clear and, after the initial pull is over, the walking is neither strenuous nor difficult. The path gains height rapidly, as you can see looking back to Rowardennan receding below. It steepens briefly, then finally zigzags to the small plateau which marks Ptarmigan's summit.

The views from here are in some ways better than those from the summit of Ben Lomond 200m above. Like many small hills, Ptarmigan offers a fine perspective on the higher peaks which surround it. The Cobbler and its neighbours are more distinctive from this lesser height. What Ptarmigan loses in distant prospects is more than made up for by the excellent view of Ben Lomond's craggy peak, its broken north-west face looking far more intimidating than it seemed from the lochside.

The name Lomond derives from *Llumnan*, the ancient Britons' word for beacon. The reason will become apparent over the next few days, when views of Ben Lomond will be a constant feature of the Highland High Way at least until it reaches Tyndrum, and in clear weather, well beyond there too.

The next part of today's route lies east along the grassy ridge which joins Ptarmigan to the summit cone of Ben Lomond. From the top of Ptarmigan, head north and then north-east. The ridge turns east as it reaches the low point of the bealach, the Gaelic word for a col or pass between two hills. Follow the path from the bealach round the rocky north-west

Ben Vorlich from Cruinn a' Bheinn

spur of Ben Lomond. The final ascent is up a broken path which climbs south to a small plateau then continues steeply to the summit trig point. The section just below the summit is rocky and eroded so care is needed, especially in bad weather. In poor visibility take care not to stray too close to the steep crags which drop away from the summit on its north-eastern side.

The views from the top of Ben Lomond are extensive, especially in the diamond-sharp light which can bless the Scottish hills in winter. It is the most southerly of the Munros and, on a clear day, you could easily persuade yourself you can see all of the 276 others. Looking north, the whole of the

Highland High Way opens up ahead of you. First comes Ben Vorlich, north-west across Loch Lomond. Beyond it at the top of the loch lie Ben Lui, Ben Oss and Ben Dubhchraig, marking the route into Tyndrum you will take in a couple of days' time. Beyond Beinn Dorain, Black Mount, Glen Coe and the Mamores beckon. The massive bulk of Ben Nevis marks the finishing point of the route. Forget Inverness, Braemar, Pitlochry and the other pretenders: Ben Lomond is the true gateway to the Highlands: a magnificent first Munro on the Highland High Way.

Of more immediate interest is the rest of today's route, lying north of Ben Lomond's summit. From here you can pick out the way across the dome of Cruinn a' Bheinn and along to the low ridge between Cruachan and Maol a' Chapuill. To continue the route, retrace your steps north to the bottom of Ben Lomond's rocky crown. From there head north-west and then north along the wide shoulder which descends to the bealach between Ben Lomond and Cruinn a' Bheinn. Keep to the high point of the ridge so that you do not lose more height than necessary. Take care in the final approach to the watershed between the Cailness burn and Caorainn Achaidh burn to avoid the rocky outcrops and cliffs which lie near the final descent. Keep left until you have crossed over them, then turn right below them to reach the bealach.

The sight of Cruinn a' Bheinn's steep slope makes it tempting to head round, rather than over, the hill. Resist the temptation. It is well worth the short climb, and in any case the terrain on the lower level is wetter and harder going. The ascent is an easy

30-minute walk and the view back to Ben Lomond, as well as west to the loch and its shoreline, is just reward for the effort.

To begin the ascent from the watershed between Ben Lomond and Cruinn a' Bheinn, head for a standing-stone prominent between two domed crests in the north-east to the right of the summit. From the standing-stone, turn north and skirt the craggy rocks to reach the top of Cruinn a' Bheinn, marked by a cairn of quartz boulders. Looking back, the route down Ben Lomond is clearly visible, bordered by the towering crags on its forbidding eastern side. Looking north, the route of the day's final climb can be seen along the bank of the burn which tumbles between Cruachan and Maol a' Chapuill.

The view across to Tarbet, with Loch Long glistening behind it, demonstrates its attraction to the Viking invaders a thousand years ago. The name Tarbet is derived from the Viking word for 'boat drag'. The village which has grown up here is one of dozens of Tarbets scattered throughout Scotland which mark a pass from one stretch of water to another where boats could be dragged through. The Loch Lomond Tarbet was used by King Haaken, the Viking leader, in 1263 as he marched his forces to the Clyde to bid for supremacy in Scotland. A fleet of 40 ships was dragged from the top of Loch Long across Tarbet to attack the communities which flourished on the islands of Loch Lomond. Haaken's ambitions were thwarted when he was defeated at the Battle of Largs and his army was forced to retreat.

As you admire the view all around, offer a small prayer of thanks. In the 1970s a reservoir and power station were proposed for this area. Had it gone ahead, most of the glen around would have been flooded and much of the surrounding area scarred with pipes and aqueducts. The plan was, fortunately, abandoned.

From the summit of Cruinn a' Bheinn, descend parallel to the deer fence heading north into Gleann Gaoithe. Keep about 10m to 20m from the fence initially to avoid the wet ground. The grassy slopes steepen sharply as you descend. Close to the bottom, a convenient wooden ramp helps you cross the fence to reach the wide expanse of the glen beyond.

For a faster descent to Inversnaid in bad weather, follow the deer fence until it meets the track which goes to Comer further down Gleann Gaoithe. Turn left on the track and follow it west to reach Loch Lomond at Cailness, from where a path along the shore goes north to Inversnaid.

To continue on the Highland High Way, go north across Gleann Gaoithe to the burn which runs down the ridge between Cruachan and Maol a' Chapuill. The floor of the glen can be very wet and boggy and it is best to keep as high as possible. A good place to aim for is an area which looks like a mine entrance, but which is in fact a spring, at the side of the track across the glen slightly to the west of the burn. A stone sheep pen at the bottom of the burn marks the point to begin the ascent.

Climb up the long grassy bank on the east side of the burn heading towards a large square boulder on the top of the ridge. It is worth pausing here to look back along the route before it disappears from view behind the ridge. Deer can often be seen here and, even if none are visible, their hoofprints in the peat are evidence of their presence.

Head for the deer fence on the ridge; cross it and follow it west towards the summit of Cruachan. Where the ridge begins to climb steeply, the small Lochan Cruachan comes into view. As it appears, turn right and head away from the fence down towards Loch Arklet and the road between Aberfoyle and Inversnaid. Descend gradually around the shoulder of the hill, keeping the rocky outcrops above you but taking care not to descend too quickly into the boggy ground around the loch.

Carry on round the slopes until the dam at the top of Loch Arklet is obscured by a small hill in front of you. Continue the descent north-west towards a pass between the hill obscuring the dam on the right and the rocky slopes rising on the left. Through the pass a low white building comes into view in the north. This is the garrison built to control the most famous inhabitant of Craigroyston, the area around Loch Lomond and the Trossachs: Rob Roy Mac-Gregor.

Part hero, part villain, Rob Roy was born in 1671 and spent the early part of his life in Glengyle and his last years at Balquhidder. But it was in this area that most of his adventures, which are now the stuff of legend, took place. Stories about him, such as Sir Walter Scott's novel *Rob Roy*, and swashbuckling movies, have intertwined fact and fiction so much it is difficult to unravel the truth of Rob Roy's life.

Scotland likes its heroes brash and rebellious and Rob Roy fitted the bill perfectly. He was a scion of the murderous Clan Gregor. The clan – even the mention of its name – was outlawed by James VI after the widows of 300 Colquhoun men killed by the MacGregors marched on Stirling brandishing their husbands' bloodstained shirts.

Rob Roy operated a successful droving business but was bankrupted by his former ally, the Duke of Montrose, and evicted from his home. Thus began a long series of raids and attacks on Montrose and his family. Rob Roy turned to cattle-rustling, robbery and blackmail – the term blackmail originates from the payments to Highland clans from livestock owners for the return of stolen black cattle or the promise not to steal cattle. Like a Highland version of Robin Hood, Rob Roy's raids were interspersed with good deeds, such as paying off an impoverished widow's debt – then stealing the money back from the debt-collector as he returned home. Despite his marauding he died peacefully in his own bed at the age of 63.

The garrison was built to keep Rob Roy and his clansmen in order, though the MacGregors did all they could to thwart its construction. They kidnapped eight of the stonemasons working on the project, but that only delayed the completion of the garrison. It was finally finished in 1713. The remains have now been incorporated into farm buildings.

Descending toward the garrison, the small spire of a church comes into view further to the west. Head down the hill towards the spire to a sheep fence. Turn left along the fence, which soon meets a taller deer fence. Follow the deer fence to a bridge across the burn, about 100m further down. The bridge is by the carpark visible through the trees on the left. Head through the trees to the carpark, then cross the bridge on to the road down to Inversnaid. From here it is a mile downhill to the hotel and bunkhouse.

Inversnaid has its own literary associations. Both Wordsworth and Gerard Manley Hopkins wrote poems about it, and Coleridge also visited it. Its fame rests partly on the pretty falls at the foot of the Inversnaid burn beside the hotel, and partly on its isolated position at the east side of the loch. Getting to Inversnaid involves either a long drive from Aberfoyle or a ferry trip across the loch; once there, though, there is little to distract from the stunning views of the loch and hills.

Accommodation on the east side of the loch at Inversnaid is limited. The hotel is a favourite stopping point for coach parties, which are ferried across from the carpark at Inveruglas on the other side of the loch. It usually has some spare rooms and it also has a small bunkhouse, which is often fully booked. The Inversnaid Lodge, to the right as you descend down the road, offers high-quality bed & breakfast. Camping is by permission of the hotel on a bivouac site south of the hotel on the lochside.

The hotel operates the ferry to the west side of the loch. It makes at least two trips daily, usually between 8 a.m. and 9 a.m., and again between 5 p.m. and 6 p.m. Non-residents can use the ferry for a small charge. The hotel reception has sailing times and sells tickets.

Accommodation is even more difficult to find on the west side of the loch. The hotel at Tarbet and hotels and campsite at Ardlui are both some distance away. You will not want to stray too far from Inveruglas, however, as it is the starting point for tomorrow's walk.

USEFUL INFORMATION

Accommodation: Inversnaid Hotel, 01877 386223.
Also has bunkhouse accommodation for 16
Inversnaid Lodge, 01877 386254

Camping: Bivouac camping available five minutes'
walk south of Inversnaid. There is also a site at
Ardlui on west side of the loch

Transport: Ferry from Inveruglas morning and
evening by arrangement with hotel
Post bus daily from Aberfoyle post office to
Inversnaid, 01877 382352

Supplies: None

Stalking: Ben Lomond – National Trust for
Scotland. No restrictions

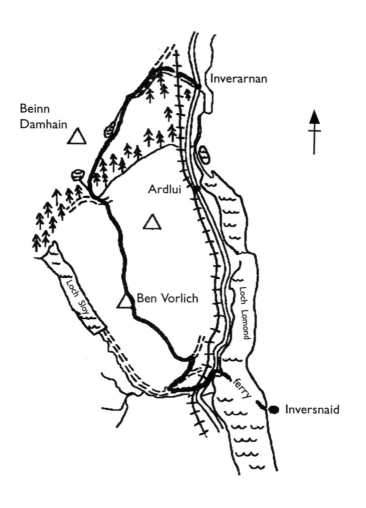

Beinn Damhain

Inverarnan

Ardlui

Loch Sloy

Ben Vorlich

Loch Lomond

ferry

Inversnaid

Day 3

Inversnaid to
Inverarnan

Day 3
Ben Vorlich

Inversnaid to Inverarnan

ROUTE SUMMARY

From the power station at Inveruglas, walk south to the dam access road. Follow the track up Ben Vorlich's eastern slope to the radio relay hut. Climb north-west to the ridge and on to the summit. Descend north to Srath Dubh-uisge then climb along the edge of the forest and turn north-east to Lochan Beinn Damhain. Continue north-east to the track through Lairig Arnan then follow the Allt Arnan down to Inverarnan.

Distance: 16km
Time: 7hr
Ascent: 1,218m
Descent: 1,204m

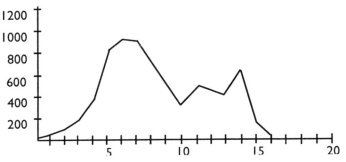

From the east side of Loch Lomond, Ben Vorlich looks imposing, even intimidating, with its sharp ridges and steep cliffs. But it is a most enjoyable climb: the ridge is broader than it appears from below and the slopes are gentler and grassier. The walk along the ridge gives a taste of the exhilarating ridge-walks which lie further north on the route.

Day 3 is relatively short. With the walk down to Inverarnan, it will take just six to seven hours. It is also a peaceful walk. Ardlui is the normal starting point for those climbing Ben Vorlich as a day's outing, and even that route is quieter than the other Arrochar Alps. Most people make Arrochar their base for a day out here and climb the more southerly hills rather than face a long walk through Glen Loin to Ben Vorlich.

The starting point for today's walk is Inveruglas on the west side of Loch Lomond. If you are staying on the east side of the loch, remember to check the sailing time of the morning ferry (usually some time between 8 a.m. and 9 a.m.) at the Inversnaid Hotel reception. Check if there will be places on board as it is a private not a public service, and there is no guarantee of a seat. The carpark at Inveruglas where the ferry docks has a snack bar, which is useful for last-minute supplies.

From the carpark it is a 10-minute walk south along the A82 road to the private track up to the Loch Sloy dam. Beware of the traffic on this road – it's the main route north to Oban and Fort William from Glasgow. Traffic is fast and the road narrow, making this an unpleasant, but brief, section.

The access road is reached just before the Inveruglas burn enters Loch Lomond, where the A82 turns sharply left. Go through the kissing gate, heeding the warnings and pausing to make a donation at the cairn for the support of local mountain rescue services – can you work out how money donated is collected from the cairn? The road goes up under the track of the West Highland Line and climbs to an electricity transmission station, 20 minutes up the hill.

The summit of Ben Vorlich is still concealed behind its steep southern ridge but there are already good views of some of the other Arrochar Alps. Ben Vane looms directly ahead. On the south side of the glen is A' Chrois with Beinn Narnain behind it.

Take the right-hand fork at the transmission station. The path turns back east and begins to climb the lower slopes of Ben Vorlich. Ignore the road which drops down to the right and instead carry on climbing until a radio relay station is reached, some 45 minutes after setting off from the carpark.

Beyond the radio relay station the road turns left round a hairpin bend to where a gated tunnel cuts into the hillside. To the left of the tunnel a clear path climbs up the side of the burn to the right of a small waterfall. The path winds north-west up the hill, with clear footholds in the bank. The climb is steep but easy going, allowing you to gain height quickly. The walk up the side of the burn gives some of the best views of the islands which pepper the southern end of Loch Lomond, as well as across to the Loch Arklet reservoir and Loch Katrine through the gap in the hills across the loch.

Like most of the burns on Ben Vorlich, and on many of the surrounding hills, this one is dammed just above 300m to feed the Loch Sloy reservoir. The effects of the diversion scheme, which channels water from an area of 80 square kilometres, are more noticeable on the descent. There, a lattice-work of dams and aqueducts takes the water back over the watershed to Loch Sloy, leaving many of the burns dry or reduced to a trickle of water.

Keeping the stream on your left, climb between two small rocky faces which appear above you. As you rise beyond them, a U-shaped gap on the ridge to the north-west above comes into view, looking like a missing tooth in the rocks. Head up the steep grassy slope and pass through the gap. This will bring you out on the south side of Coire na Baintighearna. It is worth walking a few extra metres north to admire the corrie's steep grassy bowl as it sweeps down to Loch Lomond far below. It also gives a good impression of the walk to come. The ridge curves across the western edge of the corrie rising to the summit of Ben Vorlich in the north-east. Across the corrie are the Little Hills, which conceal Ben Vorlich's summit from the loch below.

Having admired the view, go back to the top of the gap and head west. It is a short steep climb from here to the summit ridge. The Highland High Way joins the ridge close to its southern end. Loch Sloy, with the concrete dam at its end, comes into view at the bottom of Ben Vorlich's western slopes. Looking south, you can see the north peak of The Cobbler, Ben Arthur, peeping out behind the Beinn Narnain. So distinctive is its craggy, last-like shape that it can be easily identified even when only the very tip is visible. Its steep rock-faces and impressive crags make it by far the most popular of the five Arrochar Alps, despite being the only one which does not reach the magical 3,000ft needed for Munro status. The three separate rocky towers which give its distinctive shape are also the main attraction for climbers. No other hill in the southern Highlands has rock-climbs to match it, and these gave The Cobbler its place in the history of Scottish mountaineering. The country's first mountaineering group, founded in 1865, called itself The Cobbler Club. Almost a century later, the Creag Dhu Mountaineering Club pioneered routes which were, until recently, among the most difficult in Scotland.

The mica-schist rock which makes climbing on The Cobbler possible is also the dominant rock on the other Alps, including Ben Vorlich. It is at its most dramatic on the smallest hill and there are few recognised climbing routes elsewhere in the range. The Cobbler is equally accessible to walkers – and it

The summit of Ben Vorlich

is highly recommended should you wish to linger by Loch Lomond for another day. Arrochar village is the best starting point.

The ridge of Ben Vorlich is quite narrow at this south-eastern end but a well-defined path makes the walking straightforward and there is little risk of straying into the eastern corrie. The path winds gradually along the ridge heading north and north-west, occasionally dipping to skirt round rocky outcrops. There are good views from the ridge to the mountains in the west, and plenty of rocks and crags on which to sit and enjoy the view. On a clear day you can see out as far as the islands of Jura and Mull.

As the ridge undulates, climbing gradually to the summit, rocky sections alternate with broader grassy slopes. The path becomes indistinct in places but keeping to the top of the ridge is the easiest route, and will prevent you straying too far east.

After walking for half an hour along the ridge, it broadens out to a barren rocky plateau and a trig point. The true summit is a couple of hundred metres further north, marked by a cairn perched above Loch Sloy which lies 600m below.

The steepness of Ben Vorlich's western slopes, which drop almost vertically to Loch Sloy, means the reservoir cannot be seen from much of the ridge path. Though Loch Sloy may not be the most attractive loch on the Highland High Way, it is certainly valuable. Its water is used to drive the Inveruglas power station – Britain's largest hydro-electric station – on the Loch Lomond side of the hill. Water is funnelled along a 3km tunnel running through the heart of Ben Vorlich to the power station, which produces 120 million units of electricity a year. The reason for siting the power station here may be depressingly obvious if it is raining. Loch Sloy holds the mainland record for the highest rainfall in 24 hours – 238.4mm (nearly 9½ inches) on 17 January 1974. The annual average is just over 3m.

Alongside climate records, Loch Sloy does have more romantic historical associations. Its name was adopted as the battle cry of the fierce MacFarlane clan, based in Arrochar, which occupied the western slopes of Loch Lomond above Tarbet. Being on one of the main trade routes from north to south, the pickings for the MacFarlanes from robbery and rustling, were very good and close at hand. The blood-curdling screech 'Loch Sloy!' was enough to strike fear into the heart of any trader or rival clansmen. To make it even more terrifying, the clan carried out many of its raids – especially those to capture cattle from neighbouring clans – in the middle of the night. The moon is still known locally as MacFarlane's lantern, recalling those vicious raids.

From Ben Vorlich's summit cairn continue north along the ridge, admiring the views of Ben Lui and Ben Oss ahead, to reach a subsidiary top marked 931m on the Ordnance Survey map. From there the next landmark on the route is Lochan Srath Dubh-uisge, which lies above the forestry plantation north across the glen.

To descend, head north from the subsidiary top. Pick a way down the slopes, keeping slightly to the left to avoid the scattered rocky outcrops. The going is steep but not difficult, and it will take less than an hour and half to reach the floor of the glen from the summit. There is much evidence here of water management in the network of aqueducts and tunnels which criss-cross the moorland.

Lochan Srath Dubh-uisge perches above a steep brae rising north from the glen. It lies above a clear gap between two strips of forest dissected by a burn tumbling down from the lochan. Although the forests are thin and partially harvested, their regular shape makes them instantly recognisable as plantations – a useful navigational guide in poor visibility.

From Ben Vorlich head across the glen aiming for the gap between the plantations. The final part of the glen floor is best crossed on the waterworks track which begins at the aqueduct at the foot of the mountain. This is another part of the water diversion system which continues in the glens to the north.

If the weather is bad, or you intend to camp at Ardlui, it is possible to head to the A82 road from here rather than climbing to the lochan and on to Inverarnan. For the direct route to the A82, cross the deer fence at the stile and walk east along a path which runs on top of a buried water pipe for about 15 minutes. Where the path ends, descend to a ruined shieling by the burn. Follow the burn east, keeping the pylons to your right. Conditions underfoot will dictate which bank of the burn to follow, but be sure to be on the north side before it steepens to a waterfall which tumbles down to the River Falloch. The final descent should be made on the north side as the thick bracken, dense trees and a very steep slope make the south side difficult and dangerous.

As you descend towards the river, pick your way through gorse and bramble to where a red danger sign marks a ramshackle bridge over the railway. Cross the bridge and walk through the field to the

A82. Inverarnan is little more than a mile north along the busy road; Ardlui and its campsite are a shorter distance south.

To continue on the Highland High Way to Inveraran from the floor of the glen, climb between the plantations. The easiest ascent is alongside the fence which marks the edge of the eastern plantation. The ascent starts on grassy slopes but changes to peat broken by burns towards the top of the ridge. When the fence turns north-east, leave it and continue to walk north towards an eroded ridge a little way ahead. Go over the ridge at the eroded area and into a hollow which shelters a small lochan. Beyond the hollow in the north-east lies the larger Lochan Beinn Damhain. Go north-east towards the larger lochan, passing it on its southern shore. If the going is good underfoot, it will take about an hour to reach the lochan from the floor of the glen. In wet conditions the peaty terrain will make progress slower.

From the lochan continue north-east, keeping about halfway between the burn which flows out of the lochan on the left and the fence on the right. Follow the shoulder of the hill down, picking up a sheep track which runs down the ridge to the vehicle track through the Lairig Arnan. Cross the Allt Arnan by a vehicle bridge, concealed until you are almost on it. Heading for the visible western end of the vehicle track will ensure you reach the bridge. Actually, you may not need it. Courtesy of Scottish Hydro's water management scheme, the Allt Arnan is dry for much of the year. Tributaries flowing into it further down means there is usually enough water on the lower slopes of the hill to produce some pretty waterfalls on the descent to Inverarnan.

Walk a short distance along the track and leave it as it starts to climb. Instead of climbing with it, turn right off the track and follow the Allt Arnan down the slopes towards Glen Falloch. Keep to the left side of the burn where there is a faint path. On the right-hand side, the fence encroaches too close to the edge of the burn to give a sensible route.

The gurgling of the waterfalls is a pleasant accompaniment to the views east across to the Ben Glas falls and the hills above it. Ben Chabhair and An Caisteal, which lie to the north-east, are the first excursion from the Highland High Way. Both are worth climbing for the delightful approach as well as the splendid views from their summits. The excursion starts with a walk up the side of the Ben Glas falls, among the longest and most spectacular waterfalls in Scotland.

Today's descent gives one of the best vantage-points from which to view the falls. They drop more than 300m down the hill. The steepness of the terrain makes it hard to appreciate their power and majesty from the floor of the glen; but from here the full length and force of the cascade can be properly admired.

As you descend into Glen Falloch the buildings of Beinglas farm and the famous – or infamous – Drovers Inn come into view. The Drovers was a key staging-post on the droving road to cattle markets in southern Scotland and England. Over the last century it has been a favourite haunt of climbers. The Junior Mountaineering Club of Scotland frequented it in the 1930s, and tales of their exploits are legendary. On one occasion, a party driving north to Glen Coe was forced to stop by a fierce blizzard.

*The Drovers Inn, an important stance on
the old droving roads*

They failed to raise anyone at the inn, so they used
their initiative – and their ice-axes – to break in and
sleep in the bridal suite while the blizzard raged
outside. Waking up to find the weather had abated,
they continued on their way without anyone at the
inn noticing the unexpected guests' arrival or
departure.

The Drovers Inn's unusual interior and collection
of memorabilia make it a popular tourist attraction
in its own right, though it still offers accommodation
to travellers, of course. More comfortable lodgings
can be had from Ian and Nessie at the Stagger Inn
opposite the Drovers, or at Beinglas farm below the
falls on the other side of the glen. As well as bed &

breakfast, the farm has a campsite and bunkhouse accommodation in wooden wigwams. There is also a useful shop at the farm.

Follow the path from the bottom of the Allt Arnan falls to the pedestrian bridge under the railway. Go under the bridge and follow the path down to the carpark of the Stagger Inn, where the day ends.

USEFUL INFORMATION

Accommodation: Drovers Inn, Inverarnan,
  01301 704234
  Stagger Inn, 01301 704274
  Beinglas farm, 01301 704281
  Rose Cottage, 01301 704255
Bunkhouse: Beinglas farm, 01301 704281
Camping: Beinglas farm, 01301 704281
Transport: Bus from Glasgow to Fort William or
  Oban, 0990 505050
  Train from Glasgow Central Station to Ardlui,
  0345 212282
Supplies: Shops at Stagger Inn and Beinglas farm
  Campsite shop at Ardlui
Stalking: No restrictions on Ben Vorlich
Tourist Information: Tarbet, 01301 702260
  (April-October)

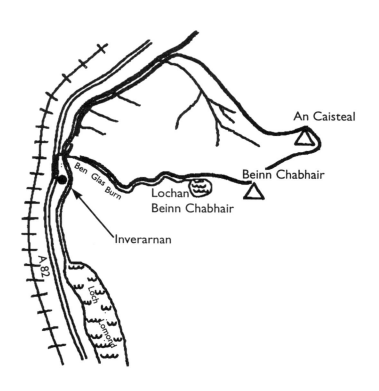

An Caisteal

Beinn Chabhair

Lochan
Beinn Chabhair

Ben Glas Burn

Inverarnan

A 82

Loch Lomond

Excursion 1

An Caisteal

Excursion 1
An Caisteal

ROUTE SUMMARY

From Inverarnan climb up the side of the Ben Glas falls and follow the path along the side of the Ben Glas burn to Lochan Beinn Chabhair. Go east to the summit of Beinn Chabhair then descend north-east to the bealach between it and An Caisteal. Climb to the ridge of An Caisteal and on to its summit. Descend over Stob Glas to the track through Glen Falloch and return along it to Inverarnan.

Distance: 19km
Time: 8hr
Ascent: 1,306m
Descent: 1,306m

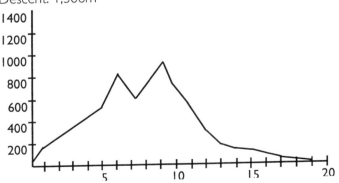

This is the first of the excursions off the Highland High Way. It is a delightful walk which is highly recommended to all those doing the route. It starts with a short, steep climb up the side of the Ben Glas burn, accompanied by the sound and sight of the waterfall which tumbles down the bank. This leads to a fine stroll through open moorland and undulating braes, with the burn still flowing alongside. The day ends with a walk back to Inverarnan by the dramatic waterfalls of the River Falloch, through coppices of birch, alder and oak. In between are two fine Munros, Beinn Chabhair and An Caisteal.

It all adds up to an excellent excursion which you can enjoy without the burden of a fully laden rucksack. The terrain is neither difficult nor particularly strenuous. A clear path takes you most of the way to the first summit, Beinn Chabhair. The ascent of the second, An Caisteal, is easier than it looks on the approach. Even the 300m drop between the two peaks is less demanding than it appears from Beinn Chabhair's summit cairn. The descent of An Caisteal's north-western ridge is over a gradual, grassy slope which leads to a good track through Glen Falloch for the final hour of the day.

The walk is enhanced by views of the steep slopes and sharp peaks of tomorrow's trio of Munros – Ben Lui, Ben Oss and Beinn Dubhchraig – which appear in the north-west as you climb to the top of the falls. Dramatic though these three hills are, the highlight of the day is the close-up view of Ben More and Stob Binnein, which look near enough to touch from the summit of An Caisteal. A return trip to climb these two striking peaks is surely a must.

Another attraction of the excursion is that it is

easy to shorten or lengthen. The route takes about eight hours, but those who want a more leisurely outing can return to Glen Falloch through Coire a' Chuilinn after the first Munro. More determined or energetic Munro-baggers can extend the day by making a detour to Beinn a' Chroin after conquering Beinn Chabhair, and then head back along the ridge to An Caisteal.

The route begins at the Drovers Inn in Inverarnan which, as mentioned in Day 3, was a traditional stopping place for drovers for centuries. Thousands of cattle were driven through Scotland by their Highland owners to trysts, or sales, at Crieff and Falkirk each year. As well as coming from the northern glens, they came from the isles, particularly Mull and Skye. The drovers moved their cattle between stances a day's walk apart. Inverarnan is the first stance encountered on the Highland High Way. Most of the stopping places from here northwards, including Tyndrum, Inveroran and Altnafeadh near Kingshouse, owe their existence to the old cattle routes.

In his classic work *The Drove Roads of Scotland*, A.R.B. Haldane estimates that, by the mid-1800s, as many as 70,000 sheep and 10,000 black cattle passed along the drove roads south to market each year. The traditional grazing fees were one shilling and sixpence – 7½p – for 20 cattle or 100 sheep. Included in the price was food for the drovers' dogs, many of whom returned alone along the route, while their owners sailed home by boat from Glasgow.

The droving route from Glen Falloch goes up gentler slopes further up the glen. The Highland High Way meets it above the Ben Glas falls and

follows it as far as Lochan Beinn Chabhair. The
drovers continued from there through the glen to
either Balquhidder or Glen Gyle and on to one of
the trysts.

To begin the day, go north from the Drovers Inn
along the A82 for 300m and cross the River Falloch
over the rickety vehicle bridge which leads to the
Beinglas farm. It is possible to buy food for the day
at the shop on the farm campsite. Otherwise, detour
round the farm on the path which links to the West
Highland Way. This goes south along the bank of the
river then east towards the falls behind the wooden
wigwams at the farm.

The path up the side of the Ben Glas burn starts
just behind the farm and climbs up the north side of
the falls. Although it looks dauntingly steep, the
long zigzags ease the climb considerably so the
ascent is not a struggle. Looking back down into the
valley, a line of trees marks the route of the canal
which used to link Loch Lomond with the Drovers
Inn. It was dug to take the pleasure steamers which
used to ply the loch right up to the hotel so that day-
trippers could stop there for lunch and afternoon-
tea. The inn and its furnishings were a bit more
genteel and in better condition at that time! There
are also good views across to the Allt Arnan which
the route followed down on yesterday's descent
from Ben Vorlich, as well as back to Ben Vorlich
itself.

After 40 minutes of steep climbing by the side of
the falls, the path levels out and crosses open
moorland. In spring, summer and early autumn the
hills glow with colour from heather, bog myrtle and

moss as well as mountain flowers like saxifrage, alpine lady's mantel and tormentil. At first a path wends its way across the moor, close to the burn, but you should stick to higher ground where the going is driest. The numerous small pools and tumbling falls on the burn are a splendid backdrop to the broad moorland and you are sure to be tempted to linger for a mid-morning break, particularly if the weather is fine.

As you leave the falls behind, Beinn Chabhair comes into view through the gap between Meall Mor nan Eag and Parlan Hill. Its summit has been hidden until now both by the steepness of the approach from Glen Falloch and by the protection of the lower hills which stand guard in the west.

Beinn Chabhair means 'hill of the hawk', and you may be fortunate enough to see a hawk. Like other birds of prey found in these hills, such as buzzards, peregrines and golden eagles, the hawk soars high above the crags, particularly those close to the Ben Glas falls. More easily spotted are smaller birds such as dotterels, meadow and rock pipits and, higher up, skylarks which spring out of the ground as you pass.

Most Scottish hills have Gaelic names and they are generally descriptive, if not always original. Knowing what their names mean can add to the enjoyment of the walk, as well as highlighting features to look out for. The second of today's peaks is An Caisteal, 'the castle', probably named after the prominent rocky knoll high up on the eastern ridge of Twistin Hill. Beinn a' Chroin, at the eastern end of An Caisteal's ridge, is one of the many 'hills of harm or danger' in Scotland, including Ben Nevis, 'venomous hill'. Dangerous hills are far outnumbered by mor (big) and beag (small) hills. The first of these seen from the route of the Highland High Way is the Crianlarich Ben More. Others, like Binnein Mor – and its inevitable neighbour, Binnein Beag – in the Mamores, follow.

Dearg (red) is also a common description for hills. The first on the route is Stob Dearg, 'red peak', which is the highest point on the Buachaille Etive Mor in Glen Coe. It is joined by Meall Dearg, 'red mound', across the glen on the Aonach Eagach. The favourite descriptions are combined in the pen-ultimate hill of the route, Carn Mor Dearg, 'big red hill' – not to mention the 'little red hill' and 'middle red hill' which lie on the same ridge.

Deer, the animal most commonly seen on the hills, are often used in the names of mountains. The noble beast is behind the most evocative name of the route, Meall a' Bhuiridh, 'hill of the bellowing of stags', in Black Mount. But there are plenty of others, including Sgurr Eilde Mor and Sgor Eilde Beag, the 'little and big peaks of the hinds' in the Mamores.

While we now call everything a hill, the Gaels were much more discriminating. Mountains could be bens or beinns, carns or ciches, stobs or sgors, mealls or mams. All signify different types of hills. Meall, for example, means mound, binnein a conical hill and stob a peak.

For the non-Gaelic speaker, pronunciation is difficult. The combinations of consonants produce sounds which are completely different to those in the English language. Today's Chabhair, for example, is pronounced *chavar*, while Meall Dearg is *myowl jerrack*. The more complicated names, like Na Gruagauchean or Beinn an Dothaidh, are real tongue-twisters. A glossary giving a translation and pronunciation guide to the main peaks on the route is included at the back of the book.

Having wandered south-east and then north-east through the glen, the path climbs up alongside the burn to its source at the Lochan Beinn Chabhair. The lochan is surrounded by high hills which, on a clear day, are reflected in its water. It is a glorious surprise to find it nestling there having completed the long walk through the glen and up the small brae to the plateau surrounding the lochan.

The path skirts north of the lochan and continues east towards the summit of Beinn Chabhair. Beyond the lochan, the path peters out. It is, however, easy to pick a route east up the steep slopes and around the rocky outcrops to the summit. Two cairns sit on separate peaks, the more easterly one marking the true summit.

From the summit, the shape of Ben Lomond in the south is instantly recognisable, even from this unfamiliar angle. To the east lie the Trossachs, including Ben Ledi and Ben Venue. Just north of the Trossachs is the other Ben Vorlich by Loch Earn. In the west, the delightfully situated Lochan a' Chaisteil makes Meall Mor nan Eag look like a volcanic crater. Beyond the lochan you can pick out Day 4's route across Ben Lui, Ben Oss and Beinn Dubhchraig. To the south-west lies Loch Long with the Atlantic and Mull visible on a clear day.

These hills were also part of the terrain of Rob Roy MacGregor. His birthplace, Balquhidder, lies off in the east. Inverlochlarig, the site of the house where he lived for a time, lies about halfway along the glen below the slopes of Beinn Tulaichean.

Ben Vorlich from the River Falloch

Of more immediate interest is the view north-east to An Caisteal and the descent to the bealach between it and Beinn Chabhair. Take heart: it is not as long a descent as it appears. The slopes of Beinn Chabhair are rocky, so care is needed, particularly on the upper section, to negotiate a way through. The climb up the other side is also shorter and less steep than it looks from this angle. It will take an hour and a half of careful walking to reach the summit of An Caisteal, from where you can admire the view back to Beinn Chabhair's rocky outline.

To begin the descent to the bealach, drop to the low col between the two cairns. From there, turn right and go carefully north-east down the steep grassy bank. As you approach the bealach, you have to weave around rocky outcrops, heading always for the path which is visible below and which winds its way up the lower slopes of An Caisteal. Take particular care on this section in snow or ice, as they can make the slopes very difficult to negotiate.

Those who want to keep the excursion day short can miss out the ascent of An Caisteal and head back to Inverarnan from the bealach. Turn north-west from the low point of the bealach through Coire a' Chuilinn, following the Allt a' Chuillin down into Glen Falloch. From there head south-west along the route of the official West Highland Way to the Beinglas farm. Although this misses out some climbing, the terrain in Glen Chuilinn is likely to be wet and boggy. The going is easier on the descent from An Caisteal.

To climb An Caisteal, follow the path from the bealach east up the lower slopes of the hill. The path ends under a large rock-face a short distance up the slope. Pass under the rock-face then turn left and make your way up the steep side of the hill to the ridge which joins An Caisteal to its easterly neighbour, Beinn a' Chroin. A detour to bag that Munro takes about 90 minutes, although the steep undulations of the ridge and the two false summits before you reach the true one, at the eastern end of the ridge, make it seem longer.

Once on the ridge a clear path heads north to An Caisteal's summit. It climbs gradually over a grassy bank, which steepens into a rocky slope, flattening out again just before the summit. At 995m, this is the highest point reached so far on the Highland High Way. The reward is excellent views east to the cone of Ben More and its table-topped neighbour, Stob Binnein. To the north-west lies Tyndrum, the next stopping-off point, with the broad slopes of Beinn Odhar and the Bridge of Orchy hills rising behind it.

A path from the summit leads north across the castle-like rocky knoll and over Twistin Hill to Glen Falloch. That route, which goes over Sron Garbh, ends up almost at Crianlarich and is a long walk back down through the glen to Inverarnan. The excursion route instead heads down An Caisteal's west ridge and joins Glen Falloch at Derrydarroch, closer to Inverarnan.

From the summit of An Caisteal, head west down grassy slopes to reach the broad rocky ridge sloping north-west to Stob Glas. Once on the ridge a path comes and goes, disappearing completely about two-thirds of the way along. Resist the temptation to take a more direct route back to Inverarnan by descending west from the ridge and following the Allt a' Chuilinn down into Glen Falloch. The lower ground is wet and boggy in all but the driest weather. Sticking to the top of the ridge as it descends over Stob Glas is a better option, more than making up in time what the lower route saves in distance.

The ridge descends across open grassy moorland. One or two gnarled trees dot the lower slopes, a tiny remnant of the ancient Caledonian pine forest. A larger, more impressive relic will be seen at the end of tomorrow's route on the lower slopes of Beinn Dubhchraig. The ridge leads to the footpath through Glen Falloch south of Derrydarroch. Turn left on the path to walk down the glen to Inverarnan.

The easier walking of the footpath will be a relief after the pathless peat and grasses of the lower slopes of Stob Glas. The pleasant woodland of Glen Falloch and the sparkling water of the River Falloch as it plunges down towards Loch Lomond provide a feast for the eyes on the stroll back to Inverarnan.

There are plenty of chances to admire the falls as they cut their deep path through the rocks. They are particularly impressive in the spring thaw. The river once flowed east towards Loch Tay and the North Sea rather than west to Loch Lomond and the Atlantic. The major land shifts which forced it to change its course also gave rise to the steep falls which make Glen Falloch the beauty spot it is today.

The path turns south just before it reaches the Beinglas farm and returns to the bottom of the falls. From there, retrace your steps back along the river to the road and on to Inverarnan.

Stalking: Glen Falloch Estate, 01301 704229

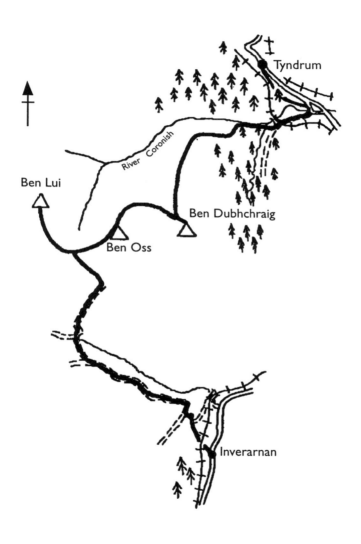

Ben Lui

River Coronish

Tyndrum

Ben Dubhchraig

Ben Oss

Inverarnan

Day 4

Inverarnan
to Tyndrum

Day 4
Ben Lui

Inverarnan to Tyndrum

ROUTE SUMMARY

From behind the Stagger Inn climb to the vehicle track that goes through Gleann nan Caorann and follow it north to its end below Ben Oss. Climb north-west to the bealach between Ben Lui and Ben Oss then head along the south ridge to Ben Lui's summit. Return to the bealach and climb Ben Oss. Continue north then east to Beinn Dubhchraig. Return to the lochans below its summit and descend to Creag Bhocan. Turn east to Dalrigh and from there take the path north to Tyndrum.

Distance: 26km
Time: 9hr 30min
Ascent: 1,827m
Descent: 1,597m

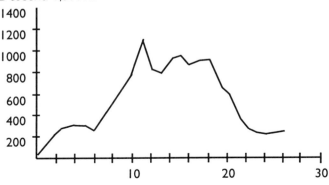

Today you leave Loch Lomond behind and head into the heart of the Highlands. The day includes two significant milestones of the Highland High Way. For the first time, the route climbs three peaks in one day, a taster of the multiple Munros which lie ahead. And Tyndrum, today's destination, marks the mid-point in the eight-day walk from Drymen to Fort William. All in all, it is a challenging but satisfying day. Ben Lui is the highest mountain on the route, pipped only by Carn Mor Dearg and Ben Nevis on the final excursion. The other two peaks today are hardly tiddlers – even the smaller, Beinn Dubhchraig, is higher than either Ben Lomond or Ben Vorlich.

The long walk in to reach the hills and the three summits climbed make it the longest day on the route so far. It is well worth the effort, though. The overwhelming feeling on the walk is one of space. First there is the wide expanse of Gleann nan Caorann with its long gentle slopes and backdrop of hills. The three Munros bagged are far enough apart to be recognisable as individual summits with views from every angle, yet close enough to give a pleasant ridge walk between them.

Each of the hills has its own charms, from the splendid views from Ben Oss's rounded summit to the rough crags of Beinn Dubhchraig, softened by the hidden jewel of Loch Oss which nestles in Coire Garbh. Ben Lui is the undisputed king of the range. Although it is only 100m higher than Ben Oss, the dramatic sweep of the ridge up to its sharply pointed summit makes it seem head and shoulders above the rest of the group. Its finest feature is the magnificent north-eastern Coire Gaothach, which plunges vertically from the summit to the glen below. A huge gorge, cradled by jagged ridges to both north and east, the corrie holds snow and ice long after winter has deserted other peaks, making it a favourite haunt of winter climbers.

Today's three hills are more commonly tackled from the north or east, avoiding the walk in from Inverarnan along the hydro-electric tracks. It is an easy and pleasant stroll, though, despite the length. The track climbs to almost 600m before it ends, leaving a straightforward walk up the grassy slopes to the col separating Ben Lui from Ben Oss. Once on the ridge, the summit of Ben Lui is little more than a step away.

The starting point for today's walk is the carpark of the Stagger Inn, opposite the Drovers, where yesterday's walk ended. Retrace your steps through the tunnel under the railway then climb north-west up the bank heading for the vehicle track about a mile ahead. Walk parallel to the line of the electricity pylons, keeping about 200m east of them.

Bracken, heather and azalea cover the slopes but it is less than half-an-hour's climb to the track. Once on the track, it is good going all the way along the south side of Gleann nan Caorann and across to the foothills of Ben Oss. The views east to the steep slopes of Ben Glas and its gushing waterfall soon disappear behind the brow of Troisgeach, but they are quickly replaced with the wide open spaces of the glen ahead.

Long grassy slopes drop from the hills to the burn, uninterrupted but for the occasional rock or solitary tree. In autumn the heathers and bracken on its slopes glow purple and orange. The colours are equally vibrant in the spring, when the emerging shoots give a fresh, yellowish-green hue. It is a great start to the day.

As you stroll up the glen, there are fine views of the hills to the west, particularly the mass of Ben Cruachan which looms into view as you round the flank of Meall nan Caora. Beinn a' Chlèibh, the fourth and smallest peak in the Ben Lui range, still manages to look impressive from this direction. It is the first to appear in the north-west but is soon joined by Ben Lui, its long south ridge climbing to a sharp summit. Next comes the rounded hump of Ben Oss standing like a bridge between the two rockier peaks on its left and right. Finally, Beinn Dubhchraig, looking deceptively craggy and steep, appears at the eastern end of the ridge.

By the side of the track there are plenty of signs of the hydro-electric scheme which draws water from the glen. Numerous small dams, aqueducts and

Ben Lui

diversion ditches cut the slopes of Meall nan Caora on the left. There are signs, too, that electricity will be joined by forestry as an economic activity of the glen. Tall deer fences section off large stretches of the bank below the track in preparation for a plantation. Enjoy the wide emptiness of the glen while it lasts.

The point where the route heads north towards the Ben Lui hills is obvious long before you reach it. The track turns right along the side of a large pipeline which cuts across the glen. Follow the pipeline as it drops to the floor of the glen then climbs to cross the Dubh Eas. At the point where the pipeline disappears into a concrete casing, a track branches off to the right over a metal bridge. Follow that track across the bridge and continue to the end of the track, about 40 minutes further on.

Keep on the track until it ends. It will feel as if you are walking away from Ben Lui but the track climbs easily over the peat hags on the floor of the glen, leaving a straightforward final pull across the lower slopes of Ben Oss to Creag Dhubh a' Bhealach and the col between Ben Oss and Ben Lui.

At the end of the path, cross the burn and climb north-west across the heather and moss slopes towards the col. Aim to pass above the small rocky outcrops which dot the slopes, as this gives the fastest route to the ridge. After about 30 minutes of climbing you will reach the bealach, a large flat plateau dotted with small lochans, peat hags and rocks. The wind whistles through it, making it feel higher and more exposed than its 700m height would suggest.

Those who want to shorten the day can miss out the ascent of Ben Lui and head directly north-east to

Ben Oss. But Ben Lui is a fine climb and it would be a shame not to do it. Both the ascent and descent are straightforward in good weather, and the round trip takes only two hours. In poor visibility you will need to use your compass, particularly on the descent, to avoid being lured south into Coire Annaich.

To climb Ben Lui, cross the col then head just west of north to climb the south ridge. The grassy slopes change to a boulderfield sprinkled with dazzling quartz as well as darker slabs which rise from the ground like gravestones. As you climb higher, views to the north open up. To the north-east Beinn Odhar and Beinn Dorain, the first of tomorrow's two peaks, are the most prominent of the Bridge of Orchy hills. Beyond them in the north are the ridges and peaks of the Black Mount.

To the south-west, a path along the ridge towards Beinn a' Chleibh shows the more common way to bag Ben Lui. To the north-east, the bright green sheds of Cononish on the floor of the glen mark the site of Scotland's answer to the Klondike. There may be no prospectors panning in the local burns but it seems there is gold in them thar hills. At the end of 1994, Stirling District Council gave planning permission for a mine here. Caledonia Mining Corporation, the Canadian company which owns the land, believes it can get more than 500,000 tonnes of gold and silver from a series of mines. The gold comes from a geological fault which runs through Scotland, crossing Beinn Chuirn on the slope you can see in the north-east. Lead and other minerals have already been extracted from the fault – old lead-workings near Tyndrum will be seen on tomorrow's route. But geological examinations over more than 200 years failed to uncover evidence of the precious yellow metal. Today's mining activity is thanks to the persistence of one geologist, Rick Parker, who spent more than ten years trying to persuade mining companies that there was enough gold to make excavation here commercially viable. While he has succeeded in that, the production of significant quantities of Scottish gold is still some way off.

A route down to Cononish and then on to Tyndrum is marked by a small cairn halfway up the ridge to the summit, close to the steep drop towards Stob an Tighe Aird. The route descends over the arm of the corrie and into its bowl and then joins the landrover track at the Allt an Rund. From there it is a straightforward one-and-a-half-hour walk along the track into Tyndrum, should you want to shorten the day.

Ben Lui's giant Coire Gaothach is hidden behind the curve of Stob an Tighe Aird almost until you reach the summit. The view when it comes is spectacular. Sheltered between two jagged ridges, the walls of corrie swoop down in a vast bowl. From the summit it is hard to believe there is any reasonable way down either of the ridges, yet both offer a straightforward scramble up from the Cononish valley when weather conditions are good. It is entertaining to sit and watch climbers negotiating their way up.

In winter the ridges above Coire Gaothach require skill in using ice-axes and crampons. A popular winter climb is directly up through the snowfields in the corrie, but this is recommended only for experienced winter climbers. The ridge at the head of the corrie often carries a wide cornice in winter and there is a risk of avalanche, particularly when the snow melts.

The cairn on Ben Lui's narrow summit is a good place from which to admire the corrie as it plummets away at your feet. It is also worth walking a little way north along the ridge to the cairn at the other side of the corrie to savour the views directly down into the massive bowl.

To descend from the summit, retrace your steps back to the bealach, taking care not to descend too far into Coire Annaich. In poor visibility the ascent of Ben Oss also needs careful navigation. The ridge to its summit is broad and featureless and it is easy to accidentally stray onto the crags to the west and east.

To start the ascent of Ben Oss, head east from the bealach for a short distance then turn north-east and finally north and scramble over the boulders which lie below the broad, barren summit plateau. It is wider than Ben Lui's slender peak. From the summit cairn, Ben Lui and Beinn Dubhchraig lie west and east respectively. The twists and curls of the ridge which joins them mean that Ben Oss is the mid-point of a lazy S-shaped curve, making Beinn Dubhchraig a longer walk away than you might think. The descent to the col between Ben Oss and Beinn Dubhchraig is straightforward, however. At its lowest point, the col is still 800m high, leaving less than 200m easy climbing to the final peak of the day.

To reach the col from the summit of Ben Oss, go north along the gently sloping ridge. The path climbs over a rocky bank, which can look as steep as a cliff in fog. From the top of the bank, the path turns

Looking across Coire Gaothach

east and descends to the low point of the bealach above Loch Oss.

From the col, Beinn Dubhchraig's western slope looks a steep climb. Appearances are deceptive, though, and just 30 minutes of easy walking lie between here and the summit. If your legs are tired, you may be tempted to miss out Beinn Dubhchraig and head north toward the Cononish river and on to Tyndrum from here. You should not: the descent through Coire Buidhe is steep and dangerous. Follow the descent outlined here even if you chose not to go as far as Beinn Dubhchraig's summit.

A clear path climbs east, steeply at first, from the col. The ridge gradually broadens out as it approaches a plateau just below the summit crest. The path skirts across the plateau, passing south of two small lochans close to the steep drop down to Loch Oss. Care is needed here, especially if the wind is sweeping through the corries. The path then climbs steeply once more to the summit cairn.

Looking back south and west along today's route, the contrast between Ben Lui's classic mountain shape and Ben Oss's rounded hump is marked. The familiar shape of Loch Lomond with Ben Lomond above it is still visible to the south-east, but for the last time on the route.

It is possible to descend directly north-east from here to the forest plantation below, but the drainage ditches there make the going slow, and the mature plantations lower down the slopes are all but impassable. Instead, head back to the lochans on the plateau below the summit. From there descend north toward Creag Bhocan, keeping to the crest of the ridge above Coire Buidhe which drops away on the left. The shoulder turns gradually east of north as the descent becomes less steep. At the bottom the slope climbs a little to a tor of rocks just before the crags of Creag Bhocan are reached. To avoid these crags, cross the fence just beyond the tor then turn east. The last section of the ridge runs east, parallel with the fence. Once on the floor of the glen, head north to the River Cononish.

The double fence on the right as you approach the Cononish river guards the Coille Coire Chuilc, one of the largest remnants of the Caledonian pine forest. The gnarled and twisted branches and the vivid green of the needles are instantly recognisable, marking these trees out as different to the younger birch and rowan trees, immeasurably more beautiful than the regimented commercial plantations.

The Caledonian pine forest once covered most of Scotland, with a tree-line as high as 300m. Despite the name, the forest was not exclusively pine; birch, oak, hazel and elm were also common there. But it is the distinctive shape of the Scots pine which is now most associated with the ancient forest.

The Caledonian forest survived for more than 9,000 years, only to be all but wiped out in a period lasting less than 500 years. Its destruction was caused by a number of factors. Initially, the trees were burnt to keep wolves away from shielings and their inhabitants. Next, baronial chiefs ordered large tracts of forest razed to destroy hiding-places for robbers and other outlaws, who used its protective cloak to hide after marauding raids. In the late sixteenth century, iron smelters moved into the Highlands and used the forest's wood to produce charcoal to fuel their furnaces. Coke took over as the main fuel in the early nineteenth century but still the fellings continued as new landlords cleared huge tracts of the glens for sheep-farming and deer-stalking. Finally, the presence of hungry sheep and deer in the glens ensured that the few trees which did remain never regenerated.

The loss of the forest changed the character of the Highlands forever. The climate and ruggedness of the area mean that it was never as fertile as lowland Scotland, and the destruction of the forests made it even less so, as the loss of the tree cover exposed the soil to erosion by wind and rain. Nowadays there are sporadic attempts to recreate the forest. The National Trust is considering replanting large sections of the land around Mar Lodge in Braemar and in parts of Glen Coe. The few ancient remnants scattered around are no longer regenerating, however, and will eventually disappear completely.

The route descends to the Cononish. If the water is low enough, cross it immediately and climb to the vehicle track on the other side. Turn right down the track and follow it for about 3km until it meets the official West Highland Way which heads north to Tyndrum.

If the river is too high to cross safely, follow the path along the southern bank to where a footbridge crosses the Allt Gleann Auchreoch, close to where it joins the Cononish. Having crossed the footbridge, take the vehicle track which winds east, making sure to cross the West Highland Railway by the closed-off vehicle bridge near where the track crosses the Cononish. Continue along the track until it joins the West Highland Way at Dalrigh.

Dalrigh was originally Dail Righ, 'king's field'. It was to here that Robert the Bruce, one of Scotland's greatest heroes, retreated after a defeat at the hands of MacDougall of Lorn. Seeing that his men were to be overtaken by the victorious clansmen pursuing them, the King ordered his men to throw their weapons into the loch so that they would not fall into the hands of the MacDougalls. Hence the name Lochan nan Arm, 'loch of the weapons', given to the small lochan at Dalrigh marked on the OS map. In the same battle, Bruce lost the brooch securing his plaid, and this remains a proud possession of the MacDougall clan.

Follow the West Highland Way path north into the forest plantation. Cross the River Fillan at the bridge which leads into the campsite and on to Tyndrum itself. There is a bunkhouse, campsite, hotels and bed & breakfasts in the village, as well as a grocer and a shop selling a range of walking equipment, from plasters to fleeces.

USEFUL INFORMATION

Accommodation: Invervey Hotel, 01838 400219
   Glengarry Guest House, 01838 400224
   Auchtertyre farm, 01838 400251
Bunkhouses: Pine Trees Leisure Park,
   01838 400243
   Auchtertyre farm, 01838 400251
Camping: Pine Trees Leisure Park, 01838 400243
   Auchtertyre farm, 01838 400251
Youth Hostel: Crianlarich, 01838 300260,
   open February to October
Transport: Bus from Glasgow to Fort William or
   Oban; train from Glasgow
Supplies: Various shops and restaurants
Stalking: Glen Falloch Estate, 01301 704229
   Forestry Commission, 01838 400254
Tourist Information: Tyndrum, 01838 400246
   (April to October)

Day 5

Tyndrum to
Bridge of Orchy

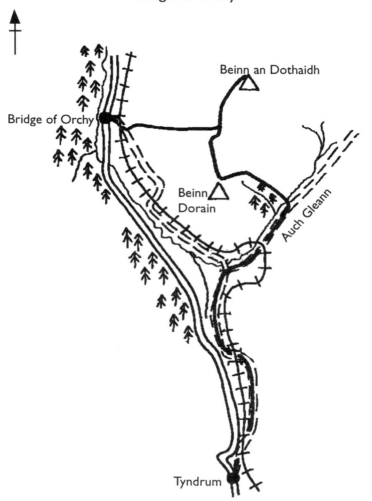

Beinn an Dothaidh

Bridge of Orchy

Beinn Dorain

Auch Gleann

Tyndrum

Day 5
Beinn Dorain

Tyndrum to Bridge of Orchy

ROUTE SUMMARY

Leave Tyndrum on the track which goes north beside the village store. Continue to Auch Gleann then turn right through the glen to Coire Chruitein. Climb up the corrie to the ridge between Meall Garbh and Beinn Dorain. Go south-west to Beinn Dorain's summit then descend north to Coire an Dothaidh. Climb north-east to Beinn an Dothaidh and return to the corrie the same way. Descend through the corrie to Bridge of Orchy.

Distance: 20km
Time: 6hr 30min
Ascent: 1,230m
Descent: 1,290m

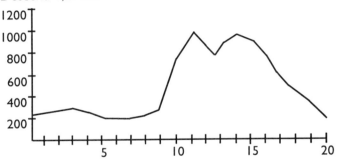

The second half of the Highland High Way is marked by another change in terrain. Just as the Highland faultline at the southern end of Loch Lomond marked the transition from the Lowlands to the Highlands, so a second faultline which is crossed at the start of today's walk marks the passage from relatively green hills to the wilder more rugged slopes of the peaks to the north.

The faultline is more than just an interesting geological feature. The mineral seams along it hastened the development of Tyndrum as a community more than a century ago, and are still affecting the local economy – as the gold-mines seen on yesterday's route testify.

Today's two hills are a potent symbol of the change in terrain. From the north and west, Beinn Dorain and Beinn an Dothaidh look like two sentries, guarding the Coire an Dothaidh between them. Approaching from the south, it is Beinn Dorain which dominates. It is a magnificent hill: the symmetry of the slopes to the right and left make it look like a massive pyramid, towering from the flat glen below. The western flanks of the hills drop 900m from their summit in long, uninterrupted slopes, broken only by the numerous burns which cut the slopes. These many burns explain the translation of Beinn Dorain, 'hill of the streamlet'.

The two hills are usually climbed from Bridge of Orchy through Coire an Dothaidh, but this is due to the convenience of parking at Bridge of Orchy station rather than the attraction of the route itself. The path through the corrie is eroded and the climb from its head to the summit undistinquished. The Highland High Way approach from Auch Gleann is more direct, although steeper, and more attractive.

This is a comparatively short day, which will be a relief after the exertion of climbing yesterday's trio of hills. Including the ascent of Beinn an Dothaidh, the walk from Tyndrum to Bridge of Orchy takes between six and seven hours.

Tyndrum means 'the house on the ridge' and comes from the national watershed which lies nearby. From here, the River Fillan heads south-east to Crianlarich then east through Loch Tay to the North Sea. A few miles away the River Lochy, which lies just west of Tyndrum, flows to the Atlantic through Loch Awe.

The route starts at the village shop in Tyndrum and follows the West Highland Way north. As the sign outside it proclaims, this is the last shop until you reach Kinlochleven, three or four days hence, so it is worth stocking up here or at the general store by the garage in the village. The latter has a selection of walking gear and a small chemist's. Tyndrum also boasts the only Little Chef on the entire Highland High Way.

The way begins as a narrow road heading north out of the village but quickly turns into a track. It winds along the flanks of first Meall Buidhe and then Beinn Odhar. Looking west on the road to Oban below the protruding nose of Sron nan Colan you can see evidence of the lead mine-workings which were once the main industry in Tyndrum, long before the town became a mecca for highland coach tour operators.

The lead ore lies on the faultline which runs from the top of Loch Fyne through Tyndrum and up to Strathspey. It brings the Dalradian schists, which

Approaching Beinn Dorain from Tyndrum

characterised the Loch Lomond hills, into contact with the quartzite rocks of the Grampian hills which run up to the Great Glen. The line marks the transition from southern to central Highlands. The Clifton mines were the most significant attempt to extract minerals from the fault, although there are various other workings along its length including the gold-workings below Beinn Chuirn, seen from Ben Lui yesterday.

Lead was discovered accidentally by Sir Robert Clifton, who gave his name to the village which grew up to service the excavations. The mines were worked from 1741 until 1862 and produced more than 5,000 tonnes of lead. At the peak of activity, they provided employment for more than 200 people, and there has been talk locally of reopening

them. Environmental sensitivity, given the importance of tourism, and dubious economics, make that
seem unlikely to happen.

Below Beinn Odhar, the route passes under the
railway through a smelly cattle creep and continues
north. Gradually the pyramid shape of Beinn
Dorain comes into view, its precipitous slopes
dominating the skyline. The gradient is, fortunately,
a little more gradual in Auch Gleann, where the
ascent begins.

An hour's stroll along the track brings you to the
bridge across Allt Kinglass which pours out of the
Auch Gleann. Turn right on the track just before the
bridge which runs alongside the burn under the
viaduct. If the water is high, it is better to cross the
burn by the bridge here and walk up the north bank,
even though there is no path on that side, as it can be
difficult to ford further up the glen.

At this point the burn tumbles over large flat
rocks, edged by small rowan and birch trees. When
the weather is fine the sights and sounds of the burn
make it a good spot to stop for a late breakfast. There
is also an excellent view of the horseshoe curve of the
railway viaduct, one of the outstanding features of
the West Highland Railway.

The railway officially opened on 11 August 1894,
just in time for the start of the grouse season on the
Glorious Twelfth. Its launch marked the culmina-
tion of more than 50 years of wrangling between
rival contenders for the route, public inquiries and
debate as well as five years of difficult and dangerous
construction work. When construction was at its
height, 5,000 people were employed, most of them
Irish navvies. The task was immense: 4,000 tons of

steel had to be transported to the Highlands to create 19 major viaducts, 102 smaller bridges and innumerable cattle creeps. It had to negotiate passes 300m above sea-level and find a way across the sodden expanse of Rannoch Moor, which was the most challenging part of the construction. The peat bogs swallowed anything laid on them – including a substantial amount of construction equipment. The solution was to float the line on a bed of turf and brushwood in the hope of creating a solid base for the sleepers. Much of it sank immediately but, eventually, enough layers were laid to provide a solid foundation. As well as the brushwood, all the soil and till used in excavating the route and 1,000 tons of ash imported from the south were used to build the foundation for the tracks. Even so, to cross the worst section of the moor, a 210m viaduct – the line's longest – had to be built.

The viaducts on the horseshoe curve may be shorter but it is still the most famous on the line. Its shape is the result of the cost pressures of the project. The shortest way across the glen is a line straight from the north-western nose of Beinn Odhar to the southern tip of Beinn Dorain. A viaduct that length would have been long and expensive to construct. The answer was to skirt the sides of all three hills, including Beinn a' Chaistell in the east, using two shorter viaducts instead of one long one.

The West Highland Railway is renowned as one of the most scenic rail routes in the world. It runs for 165 miles from Glasgow to Fort William and on to Mallaig, with a branch going to Oban from Crianlarich. The early trains took five hours to get from Glasgow to Fort William. More than a century later, the journey time on a good day is only an hour less. The glory of the scenery it passes through, from Loch Lomond to Loch Tulla, Rannoch Moor to Glen Falloch, and particularly the Fort William to Mallaig section, means passengers are more likely to find the journey too short than too long.

John Thomas's book, *The West Highland Railway*, is a lively account of the line's origins and contains many anecdotes of its early years. On one occasion a train, appropriately called The Ghost, slowed at Corrour to pick up some freight. It accelerated sharply as the pick-up was completed, just at the point where the line drops steeply downwards. The brake van at the back of the train was so jolted by the sudden burst of speed that it uncoupled and rolled back down the line, with the guard fast asleep on board. From Corrour, it is downhill for the 25 miles back to Bridge of Orchy. The rogue van gathered speed and raced down the track. Railwaymen on the line tried to stop the runaway but its gathering speed – and their concern for the safety of the guard – forced them to allow it to continue its downward path. The stationmaster at Bridge of Orchy eventually caught up with it close to this point. When it came to a halt, the guard was still soundly asleep in the back.

The book also records the effect of fierce Scottish winds on a train's progress. In 1962, a train heading round the horseshoe to Fort William slowed from 35 miles an hour to 15. The driver thought a passenger had pulled the communication cord, but eventually discovered it was the impact of the headwind blowing down the glen from the west.

Just before you pass under the viaduct, you meet

a ford made from concrete railway sleepers across the Allt Coralan. When the water is low the ford can be easily crossed; otherwise go south to cross the burn where it narrows. Carry on under the viaduct and round into the vast empty Auch Gleann which heads into Glen Lyon. Auch is short for Ach-innis-chalean, 'field of hazel meadow'. It once held a royal hunting-lodge, patronised by James IV, and its owners were required to supply venison for royal feasts.

Half-an-hour's walk along Auch Gleann brings you to a small plantation to the left of the path which marks the bottom of Coire Chruitein. Cross the burn just after the plantation and climb the vehicle ramp to reach the bottom of Beinn Dorain's southern slope. The route up the grassy slopes to the rocks and crags at the top of the corrie is clear above you. The long slog up to the ridge will get the calf muscles singing and the lungs working but, once the ridge is reached, it is an easy stroll south-west to the summit.

Keeping the trees on your left, head up the steep grassy slope aiming for the plantation's top corner. Beinn Dorain's rich and fertile mixture of mica-schists and limestone means the grassy banks are often dotted with yellow tormentil, blue milkwort and the pinkish-red lousewort as well as the glorious purples and yellows of saxifrage. As you climb, the three peaks of yesterday's route – Beinn Dubh-chraig, Ben Oss and Ben Lui – come into view behind you to the left. Across the glen in the south, the steep sides of Beinn a' Chaisteil look no more accessible than they seemed from the glen below.

When you reach the top of the plantation, strike

Along the summit to Beinn Dorain

off to the north, keeping the burn about 200m on the left. Aim for the small ridge directly above you. The grassy slopes steepen as you approach the ridge and wind between rocky outcrops, easing as the ridge is gained.

As you might have expected, this is not the summit ridge. That lies above the grassy plateau just above the rocky headwall of Coire Chruitein off to the west. The most direct route to the summit lies west across this grassy plateau. A spring halfway across it, just below a short scree slope, gives beautifully cold water even on the hottest day.

In poor visibility it is easier to head directly north to the summit ridge, which requires only a little easy scrambling at the top. That reaches the ridge on the flat top near to the cairn marking Meall Garbh's summit.

The ridge gives the first views east towards the vast cauldron of Coire a Ghabhalach, the twin of the Coirean Dothaidh above Bridge of Orchy. More impressive even than the corrie is the panorama which opens up to the north-west. The unmistakable hulk of Ben Nevis rises over the Mamores across Rannoch Moor. As you progress south-west along the ridge towards the summit, views down Glen Orchy, with Ben Cruachan and Loch Awe beyond, open up. To the south-east, the table-top of Stob Binnein behind the bulk of Ben More is as distinctive as ever.

A path heads south-west along the ridge towards Beinn Dorain's summit, turning from grassy bank to boulderfield. It skirts round the corrie, whose rocky sides drop steeply from just below the summit. A well-built igloo-shaped cairn marks the point where the ridge joins the route up from Bridge of Orchy. This can easily be mistaken for the summit cairn in poor visibility but the true top lies 200m south, reached by a path which first drops a little then climbs again to the real summit cairn. Descend a little way south from the summit for a good view back to the first half of today's route, dominated by the graceful horseshoe curve of the railway on the floor of the glen 900m below.

It is easy to appreciate why Beinn Dorain was such an inspiration for one of Scotland's greatest poets, Duncan Ban Macintyre, 'fair-haired Duncan of the songs'. He was born in 1724 near Loch Tulla and was for many years gamekeeper to the Earl of Breadalbane. His first book of poems was published in 1768, transcribed by a clergyman friend from oral recitation. Macintyre had had no schooling and had never learned to read or write. He spent much of his time deerstalking in the hills around the area. Beinn Dorain was his favourite. His most famous poem, one of the finest in the Gaelic language, is called *Beinn Dorain* and records his love for its slopes. A vivid account of the colours and scenery of the hill, and the deer which roam around its slopes, it proclaims:

Honour past all bens
to Ben Dorain
of all beneath the sun
I adore her.

As evocative is *The Last Adieu to the Hills*:

Yestereen I stood on Ben Dorain and paced its
*   dark grey path.*
Was there a hill I did not know? a glen or grassy
*   strath?*
Oh! gladly in the times of old I trod that glorious
*   ground.*
And the white dawn melted in the sun, and the red
*   deer cried around.*

Macintyre married the daughter of the landlord of the Inveroran Hotel on the shore of Loch Tulla which the Highland High Way passes later in the route. Despite his passion for the hills, he left them later in life to move to Edinburgh where he took the unlikely job of policeman. He died there in 1812.

From the true summit of Beinn Dorain, retrace your steps to the large igloo cairn and continue north down the path towards the col which marks the top of Coire an Dothaidh. The well-worn path broadens out, becoming extremely eroded and steep in places as it heads downwards. In poor visibility the curve of the terrain could lead you east and it is worth taking a compass-bearing to avoid making that error. The terrain offers some clues to the descent as the path down is eroded and worn, in contrast to the grassy slopes which fall away to the east.

The path heads towards two small lochans above Coire an Dothaidh. At the largest of these, just above the corrie, the path turns sharply right to skirt around the lochan. It then turns north again to descend to the head of the corrie, marked by a tiny lochan and another cairn. A path continues down into the corrie and descends to Bridge of Orchy.

If the weather is poor, or if the day has been long enough, you may decide to head down the path instead of taking in Beinn an Dothaidh. If you have the energy, however, it is well worth going to that summit for the excellent views across Loch Ba and Rannoch Moor towards Schiehallion. Although the slopes look steep and the summit (the middle of the three peaks you can see) some way off, it takes less than an hour to climb up and back.

The path up Beinn an Dothaidh climbs east from

Bridge of Orchy

the col. It eventually peters out and the route continues north-east up the grassy bank to the summit. A small cairn marks the point from which to start the final climb. Aim for the ridge between the centre and western peaks as this avoids the worst of the boggy ground below the summit.

The summit cairn is distinguished by a white marble centrepiece. From here there are good views across to Beinn Achaladair and Beinn a' Chreachain, the highest of this group of hills, behind it. Off to the north-east are some fine views of the barren expanse of Rannoch Moor, which will be a feature of the route for the next three days.

From Beinn an Dothaidh, Beinn Dorain looks a completely different hill. There is no hint of the shapely cone which makes it so distinctive on the approach from Tyndrum. Instead, it is a long ridge leading up to a featureless top. The view is distinguished by a spectacular waterfall tumbling down broken crags to the left of the summit, the sound reverberating across the hills when the burn is in spate.

To descend, head west along the ridge to Beinn an Dothaidh's western top. From here, there are splendid views across to Loch Tulla and Black Mount beyond. Turn south and descend to the left of the hill's shoulder. Pick up the path again near the cairn where you started the final ascent. Do not stay on the ridge all the way back to the col as there are steep, dangerous rock walls just before the col.

Return to the col between the two Munros and from there head west into Coire an Dothaidh. The path through the corrie is steep and badly eroded in places and its lower sections quickly become very boggy after rain. The slopes to the left and right are scattered with huge boulders.

A distraction from the descent is the view across to Loch Tulla and Black Mount. On a fine day, when the waters of the loch take on the clear blue of the sky, it provides a stunning contrast to the lush green of the moor and hills surrounding it.

The descent gradually eases and the day ends with an easy stroll down to Bridge of Orchy. The hotel there has a bunkhouse. There are places to camp over the bridge on the riverbank and a couple of houses offering bed and breakfast. The West Highland Railway also stops here.

Bridge of Orchy is another traditional droving stance. The bridge over the River Orchy just behind the hotel dates back to about 1742 and is a scheduled ancient monument, described as 'segmental arch random rubble'. Its main claim to fame is a starring role in *John Splendid*, one of the two novels by Neil Munro to be set in this area.

You can end today's route either here or at the Inveroran Hotel, two miles away over Mam Carraigh. Inveroran is closer to Black Mount, crossed on tomorrow's route, but there is a wider choice of accommodation at Bridge of Orchy.

USEFUL INFORMATION

Accommodation: Bridge of Orchy Hotel,
01838 400208
Inveroran Hotel, 01838 400220
Glen Orchy farm, 01838 200221
Mrs J. MacDonald, Fir Park Auch, 01838 400233
Bunkhouse: Bridge of Orchy Hotel, 01838 400208
Camping: by Bridge of Orchy and
Inveroran hotels
Transport: Train from Glasgow Central,
0345 212282; bus from Glasgow, 0990 505050
Supplies: Small shop and post office by the railway
station
Stalking: Auch Estate, 01838 400269
Tourist Information: Tyndrum, 01838 400246
(April to October)

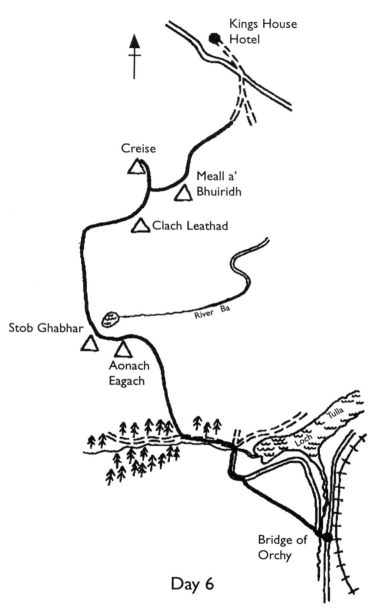

Kings House
Hotel

Creise

Meall a'
Bhuiridh

Clach Leathad

River Ba

Stob Ghabhar

Aonach
Eagach

Tulla

Loch

Bridge of
Orchy

Day 6

Bridge of Orchy
to Kingshouse

Day 6
Black Mount

Bridge of Orchy to Kingshouse

ROUTE SUMMARY

At Victoria Bridge follow the track west along Abhainn Shira. Go north along the path through Coire Toaig and south up to the Aonach Eagach. Follow the ridge to Stob Ghabhar then head north along the Aonach Mor, crossing to climb Clach Leathad at the Bealach Fur-chathaidh. From Clach Leathad's summit, head north to Creise then return south to the bealach across to Meall a' Bhuiridh. Descend north to the ski carpark and along the road to the Kings House Hotel.

Distance: 24km
Time: 9hr 30min
Ascent: 1,748m
Descent: 1,678m

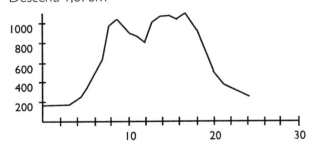

The route from Inveroran to Kingshouse across Black Mount is one of Scotland's classic hill-walks. In 11 miles (18km) it takes in three Munros, three other tops and a climb of more than 1,700m. It is an excellent introduction to the ridge-walking which is a feature of the route from here onwards. While parts are narrow and steep, the walking is excellent and the views all around are spectacular.

Black Mount is actually a range of hills stretching from the edge of Rannoch Moor in the east to Ben Starav in the west. The name originates from the moor which lies to its east rather than from the peaks – 'mount' in Scotland traditionally meant moor – but is now applied to the range of hills. It includes 14 tops and some spectacular corries, including Coireach a' Ba and the precipitous Coirean Lochain, a fine example of a hanging corrie.

Today's route covers the best of Black Mount. It starts by scaling the Aonach Eagach – a rather less intimidating ridge than the more famous one on the next stage of the Highland High Way – and climbing Stob Ghabhar. It continues over a series of broad ridges and bealachs to conquer Clach Leathad and Creise. It ends with the highest hill in the Black Mount, the evocatively named Meall a' Bhuridh, 'hill of the bellowing of stags'. It takes in narrow arêtes and wide grassy banks, rocky boulderfields and slippery scree. There are spectacular views: the long, open vistas across Rannoch Moor; the angular ridge of Buachaille Etiνe Mor, with its uncompromising buttresses at either end; and most pleasing, the hills of the Black Mount itself.

In good weather, it is a long and satisfying day although even in perfect visibility the ridges which span out from Stob Ghabhar can be confusing. In poor visibility navigation can be a problem at several key points – especially finding the Bealach Fuar-chathaidh which joins the Aonach Mor to Clach Leathad, and the ridge linking Creise with Meall a' Bhuiridh. The route should not be attempted in winter unless you are experienced in snow- and ice-climbing.

Beginning at the Inveroran Inn cuts out a long walk at the start of the day. That will mean either taking a room at the hotel or camping somewhere along the road beside it. Signs by the hotel ban camping but there is a pleasant spot for rough camping a few minutes further along the road towards Victoria Bridge. The nearest bunkhouse is at Bridge of Orchy, back at the foot of Beinn Dorain. From Bridge of Orchy, you can choose either to go along the road by the side of Loch Tulla, or to climb over Mam Caraigh, following the route of the official West Highland Way. Although a mile shorter, the latter is often wet and boggy; the tarmac road is easier going.

In good light it is possible to make out the parallel 'roads' on the hills above Achallader farm at the east end of Loch Tulla. Like the more famous examples in Glen Roy above Fort William, these are a product of the last Ice Age. They identify the sites of ancient lochs, formed when ice from the glaciers plugged exit routes for the water. As the glaciers retreated, the ice plugs disappeared and the level of the lochs lowered, leaving a series of beaches or parallel roads in their wake.

A remnant of the Caledonian pine forest can be seen at Doire Darach, where the Marchioness of

Breadalbane fenced the trees in to protect them from sheep and deer – with evident success. The experiment has been repeated at various other sites around Rannoch Moor, returning some of the moor to its original wooded state, and introducing a more natural forest with a variety of trees than the unrelenting acres of spruce and fir characteristic of Forestry Commission plantations.

Inveroran was a key cattle stance for drovers travelling south from Glen Coe and Skye. The stances were established a day's walk apart, where drovers could rest and graze their cattle as they herded them to trysts further south. Inveroran's importance was made clear in a court case against Lord Breadalbane in 1844. He wanted the stance moved to Tyndrum, freeing the land for deer, but the drovers felt this was too far to walk from the preceding stance at Altnafeadh at the end of Glen Coe. The Court of Appeal agreed and insisted that a stance be maintained at Bridge of Orchy. Even today, the tenant of Achallader farm at the end of Loch Tulla has to keep the droving stance open under the terms of his lease – handy if you want to bring a herd of black cattle with you on holiday!

Lord Breadalbane's family seat, Black Mount Lodge, lies on the north side of Loch Tulla. At the start of this century one of its residents was the Marchioness of Breadalbane whose book, *The High Tops of the Black Mount*, is an entertaining account of her days spent walking and hunting in the hills. The Breadalbanes seem to have been a colourful family. Another in the line, the Marquess, formed the Black Mount Literary Association at Achallader Camp 'to excite a spirit of inquiry combined with healthy amusement' in the navvies who built the West Highland Railway between Glasgow and Fort William.

From Inveroran the day's route continues along the road to Victoria Bridge, where the Highland High Way parts company with the West Highland Way. The gnarled shapes of the Caledonian pines enhance the tranquillity of the loch – a sharp contrast to the eastern side, by the A82 road, where maturing plantations block the loch from view. In the early morning, curlews with their distinctive curled beaks and plaintive cry rise from the shore.

Victoria Bridge was almost chosen as the site of the royal family's Highland summer retreat instead of Balmoral on Deeside. It was visited by Queen Victoria when she was searching for a Highland home. She may have been put off by the weather: Rannoch Moor is one of the wettest parts of Scotland, with average annual rainfall of more than 3m.

At the forest lodge just beyond Victoria Bridge, turn west along the track marked with a green finger sign pointing the way to Loch Etive via Glen Kinglas. This is a fine low-level walk for another day.

From the lodge, follow the vehicle track along the north side of the Abhainn Shira for 20 minutes. This is a lovely glen. It is bounded by hills on virtually all sides but they are distant enough to give a feeling of space, yet close enough to be pleasing on the eye.

The ascent of Black Mount begins at the green corrugated hut a mile down the glen. This now belongs to the Glasgow University Mountaineering Club, but was once a schoolhouse – the Marchioness of Breadalbane writes of joining a lesson in its

Heading up Coire Toaig

'primitive' classroom. Its existence is evidence that the area's population was once larger than it is now.

A path climbs north towards Coire Toaig from the schoolhouse, gradually at first following a straight route through the corrie. Exposed tree roots in the drainage ditches by its side show how thick the Caledonian forest once was. The oldest roots on Rannoch Moor date back more than 7,000 years. As it enters the corrie, the path begins to climb more steeply, twisting and turning up the right-hand side of the burn.

About two-thirds of the way to the head of the corrie, a path branches away to the right and zigzags up the southern flank of Stob a' Choire Odhair. If you have the stamina, and the confidence that there will be enough daylight to finish the route safely, you can detour up here to bag the Munro. It is a long diversion on an already full day.

The Highland High Way continues, climbing steeply but steadily through the corrie with the burn on the left, the path fading as it reaches the top of the corrie. The view from the ridge at the top is outstanding and it is worth the short walk to the edge of the corrie to appreciate it. First to grab the attention are the grey, glacier-scarred walls of Coirein Lochain as they plunge vertically to the lochan far below. To the east lies Rannoch Moor, its flatness framed by the steep walls of the Coire Dhearbhadh. At the top of the corrie wall in the west lies Stob Ghabhar, its rocky ridges and crags making it look a far more daunting climb than it actually is.

Rannoch Moor is one of Britain's last great wildernesses. It is a vast basin of granite over 60 miles square and more than 400 million years old. It was gouged out by a sheet of ice up to 1,100m thick during the last Ice Age. The defining feature is its flatness – in the 13 miles from the Ba Bridge at the foot of Black Mount to Rannoch Station, the drop is just 44m. The going may be flat but it is not easy. The granite bed gives poor drainage, as can be seen in the myriad of lochans, pools and streams which criss-cross the ground. The poor drainage means the moor is a morass of bogs and peat hags, making slow, heavy going for the walker.

The wet ground is not the only hazard. The moor is featureless and navigation difficult. One of the best illustrations of this is the adventures of a party of men surveying the route for the West Highland Railway in January 1889. Seven men, including the builder Robert McAlpine (who was later knighted), set off from Spean Bridge heading for Inveroran 40 miles away. The trip was beset with difficulties from the start. An oarsman who was supposed to row them across a loch to the hunting-lodge where they

Coirein Lochain

were to stay overnight turned up late and their passage was then hindered by appalling weather. They did not reach the lodge until after midnight. Undeterred, they set off the following day to a prearranged meeting halfway across the moor. With just three hours of daylight left and 14 miles still to go, three of the party decided to stop and stay with the seventh member who was too exhausted to continue. The other three pressed on, eventually reaching their destination.

The three who remained on the moor danced around in circles to keep warm, only to lose sight of their exhausted colleagues. They set up a makeshift shelter with one of their umbrellas to mark the sick man's position. Their relief at being rescued, at 2.30 in the morning, was immense.

On a sunny day the moor looks glorious. The pools and lochans glint in the sunshine lighting up the purples, greens and oranges of the heather, peat and bracken. The conditions make it a haven for wildlife and a favourite haunt of botanists and ornithologists. It is the home of many rare birds and plants including the Rannoch rush which is not found anywhere else in Britain.

Having savoured the views from the head of Coirein Lochain, continue on the route as it climbs steeply up the north slope of the Aonach Eagach. Follow the path south which zigzags across scree and rocks. The slope is steep and eroded in places but there are plenty of foot- and handholds making it an easy scramble to the ridge. The path is clearer than it looks from the bottom of the scree slopes and it only takes 30 minutes to reach the top of the Aonach Eagach.

On reaching the ridge, a fine panorama of the route opens up to the north, views that improve on the summit of Stob Ghabhar a short walk away. The first section of the ridge is rather narrow and craggy, a foretaste of what awaits on its namesake at the other side of Glen Coe. It is short, however, and the ridge quickly broadens out to a wide grassy bank which heads west and then north-west to Stob Ghabhar.

Less than 30 minutes along the ridge lies the cairn which marks Stob Ghabhar's summit. Looking back, you get a good view of the previous two days of the route. Trains on the West Highland Railway chug steadily round the flanks of Beinn an Dothaidh and Beinn Dorain. Further south is the trio of Ben Lui, Ben Oss and Beinn Dubhchraig. But your eyes are likely to be kept firmly on the route ahead by the broad stretch of Aonach Mor and the steep rocky slopes of Clach Leathad in the north.

In between them in the background Buachaille Etive Mor guards the entrance to Glen Coe. The view from Kingshouse may be more dramatic, but from this point you can really appreciate the hill's length and stature.

A line of fence posts, which started at the base of the final climb to the summit, heads off along Stob Ghabhar's westerly ridge towards Stob a Bhruaich Leith. The curve of the hill may tempt you to head off in that direction in poor visibility but the route lies north above the western wall of Coirein Lochain initially, then turns north-west to join the aptly named Aonach Mor, 'big ridge'.

As you descend to the Aonach Mor from the summit of Stob Ghabhar you leave behind the gneiss rocks of the first part of the route and meet the pink and grey Cruachan granite which underlies the rest of today's route. The shift is marked by a change in the vegetation from grassy slopes to the boulder-fields which are a feature of the day's remaining tops.

The descent from Stob Ghabhar needs careful compass work in bad weather. Keeping to the edge of the precipice on the right takes you in the correct direction initially, but staying with it too long takes you along Sron nan Giubhas instead of along Aonach Mor. Head north initially until the ridge starts to turn off eastwards to the steeply walled Sron nan Giubhas. At that point, head north-west to the wide ridge, the Aonach Mor.

Careful navigation is needed to find the Bealach Fuar-chathaidh which crosses to Clach Leathad. In poor visibility this is extremely difficult. The point where the bealach leaves the ridge lies about a 50-minute walk from the summit of Stob Ghabhar. The ridge undulates and there is no easy way of identifying the bealach. A cairn marks the spot to turn north-east on to the bealach but the cairn is small and the ridge wide, making it easy to miss.

If you do miss it, an alternative route to the hotel at Kingshouse can be found by continuing along the Aonach Mor and descending its north-west shoulder. At the meeting point of two burns which flow down from either side of the ridge there is a stalkers' path which leads down to Alltchaorunn in Glen Etive. The bridge across the River Etive bristles with barbed wire but you should be able to find your way across. Turn right up the road and it is an hour's walk to Kingshouse.

Rannoch Moor from Black Mount

To cross the bealach to Clach Leathad, drop down to the left to avoid the worst of the boulderfield which lies beneath Aonach Mor. Head across the bealach to the slopes of Clach Leathad looming at the other end. There are outstanding views down through Coireach a' Ba to the loch and moor beyond. This translates as 'corrie of the cattle', named because of its use as a shelter for cattle as the drovers made their way down to the next stance at Inveroran. The Marquess of Breadalbane summed up its grandeur with the words: 'Nothing can be more inspiring or magnificent than the aspect of this

great corrie, flanked on all sides by towering heights, tenanted in solitary glory by the red deer who have roamed at liberty there for centuries.'

Black Mount is still one of the great hunting estates and it is quite likely that you will see herds of deer here. There are also black grouse, distinguished by the red plume on their heads. Their slowness along the ground makes it possible to get quite close to them before they make their escape.

Coireach a' Ba demonstrates the unusual drainage patterns of the Black Mount. Although less than ten miles from the Atlantic in the west, much of the

Meall a' Bhuiridh

Black Mount drains to the North Sea away in the east. The Ba burn starts just below the bealach and joins the sea at the Firth of Tay in Dundee, having flowed over Rannoch Moor and through Loch Tulla, Loch Rannoch and Loch Tay on its way across Scotland.

The climb up Clach Leathad is something you could probably do without at this stage in the day. Close up, it is every bit as steep as it looked from the other side of the bealach, but half an hour's climb should get you up to the ridge which leads to the summit. There is no clear path off the bealach to the ridge and it is as well to head directly upwards. Once there, the derivation of Clach Leathad, 'stone of the broad slope', is clear. The wide ridge which leads to the summit cairn and bad-weather shelter is strewn with broken granite boulders that become smaller and smoother closer to the top. From the ridge, the route carries on east then north-east to the summit cairn, perched above the steep bowl of Coire an Easain.

In Sir Hugh Munro's original tables, Clach Leathad (pronounced 'Clachlat') was the Munro; Creise, further to the north, was simply designated as a top. Creise, a full two metres higher at 1,100m, has since been promoted to the Munro while Clach Leathad has been demoted to a top. Creise still does not merit inclusion in the OS map, however; it is identified only by its height.

From Clach Leathad, the route goes west briefly then north down a rocky slope to the ridge along to Creise. The bealach across to Meall a' Bhuiridh arcs off to the right in a huge symmetrical curve which looks as if it is marking the path of a giant pendulum.

The bealach is before Creise's summit, but Munro-baggers will want to carry on up the path to the summit, a 30-minute detour there and back, before heading across to Meall a' Bhuiridh.

Meall a' Bhuiridh is the shapeliest hill on today's route and this is the best angle from which to appreciate it. It looks like a slender pyramid, balancing gracefully atop a narrow ridge – a much more attractive prospect than the ski-ravaged slopes seen above Kingshouse.

Locating the bealach to Meall a' Bhuiridh can be difficult in poor visibility. The cairn marking the descent to this bealach is a decent size and lies at the edge of the side of the path, so is a better guide than the one on Aonach Mor. A clear path climbs down rocky slopes to the bealach. The way is steep enough to need care in poor conditions. The bealach is also very exposed and there can be a noticeable wind even on a calm day; on a windy day, the gusts can be strong enough to make the going very difficult indeed. It is, however, an exhilarating walk with good views of the corries to both left and right.

The climb up to Meall a' Bhuiridh's rocky summit is straightforward. From there you can recap on the day's conquests as well as looking forward to your destination in Kingshouse. Head north from the summit cairn where a path winds down the slopes to the ski area on the plateau below. The White Corries ski lift opened in 1960, the first chairlift in Scotland. The tow is open most of the year for sightseers as well as skiers. If your legs are tired, you can hitch a lift down to miss out the last part of the descent.

To walk down from the top of the chairlift, follow the path of wooden steps and split logs to the derelict building which marks the place where the old chairlift ended. A path 20m to the right of the old buildings zigzags down to the carpark below. From there the old military road crosses the A82 and continues to the Kings House Hotel. Blackrock cottage, about halfway between the carpark and the A82, belongs to the Ladies Scottish Climbing Club.

Kingshouse is also the site of a long-established drovers' stance, and is now the home of Glencoe Mountain Rescue. As well as accommodation in the hotel, it is possible to camp by the side of the hotel.

USEFUL INFORMATION

Accommodation: Kings House Hotel,
   01855 851259
Camping: Rough camping at the back of the hotel
Transport: Bus from Glasgow or Fort William,
   0990 505050
Supplies: None
Stalking/sheep: Hamish Menzies, Black Mount
   Estate, 01838 400225
Tourist Information: Fort William, 01397 703781

Excursion 2

Buachaille Etive Mor

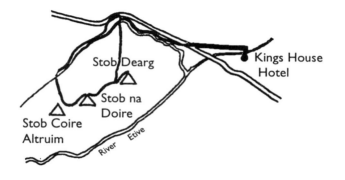

Stob Dearg

Stob na Doire

Stob Coire Altruim

River Etive

Kings House Hotel

Excursion 2
Buachaille Etive Mor

ROUTE SUMMARY

Take the path from the A82 along the River Coupall to Lagangarbh. Climb through Coire na Tulaich to the ridge then east along the path to Stob Dearg. Return to the col and continue west then south-west to Stob na Doire. From the col before Stob Coire Altrium descend into the Lairig Gartain. Follow the track through the Lairig Gartain back to the A82 and retrace your steps to the Kings House Hotel.

Distance: 19km
Time: 8hr
Ascent: 923m
Descent: 923m

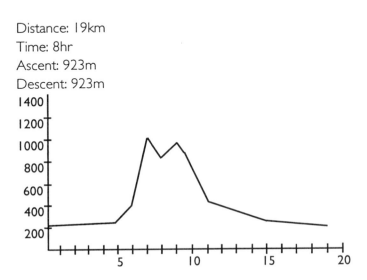

Buachaille Etive Mor is *the* mountain of Glen Coe. The Pap of Glencoe may be more symmetrical, the Three Sisters more forbidding and Bidean nam Bian higher, but it is the majestic pyramid of Buachaille Etive Mor, guarding the eastern gateway to Glen Coe, which symbolises the wild, uncompromising atmosphere of the glen itself. It is a spectacular sight. W.H. Murray, climber and author of some classic Scottish travel guides, described it as 'the most splendid of earthly mountains'. Admiring it from the Kings House Hotel, the finest and most famous aspect, it is hard to disagree. In the late evening sun, its rhyolite buttresses glow pink, illustrating why its highest top is called Stob Dearg, 'red peak'. Even such gentle light cannot hide the fact that it is the most impenetrable of hills. The nearer you are, the more forbidding it becomes. From a distance it looks like a solid wall of rock; close to, the huge folds, gullies and buttresses carved out of the rock stand out in sharp relief. It is these features which make it a mecca for rock-climbers, who cling ant-like to its steep faces in both summer and winter.

The Buachaille was one of the early centres of Scottish climbing. Although the Chasm, a huge gash on the Glen Etive side of the hill, has now been superseded by the Clachaig Gully on the Aonach Eagach as the longest gully climb on the mainland, features like the Crowberry Tower and Raven's Gully, and climbing routes like the January Jigsaw and the Devil's Cauldron, mean the Buachaille still ranks as one of Scotland's favourite climbing hills.

All this does not mean it is inaccessible to walkers, though – indeed, compared to the long climbs on some of the other hills on the Highland High Way so far, the ascent in good weather is short and straightforward. There is, however, little choice about how to do it – and in snow, the sensible decision would be not to do it at all unless you are experienced in winter climbing and are aware of the risks of avalanches. The Buachaille has claimed the lives of many climbers in winter.

The walkers' route is a scramble through Coire na Tulaich on the Buachaille's northern side. This starts as the A82 road heads into Glen Coe proper. The corrie is steep and boulder-strewn but it is possible to reach the ridge with a minimum of scree-scrambling, and only a little rock-hopping. In winter a large snow cornice forms at the top of the corrie, which makes climbing up or down it difficult and dangerous. In poor visibility, navigating the route up to the summit – and, more importantly, back down to the head of the corrie – can also be very difficult.

Today's route takes in Stob Dearg, the summit seen from the Glen Coe road, and continues halfway along the Buachaille's ridge. It descends on the eastern side of the ridge to return to Kingshouse through the dramatic Lairig Gartain. Taking in some of the other tops on the Buachaille's long ridge, instead of just bagging its Munro, makes for a very enjoyable walk as well as offering a different perspective on its cliffs and corries. It also gives fine views across the other Glen Coe peaks and south into Glen Etive.

To reach Coire na Tulaich, take the road west from behind the Kings House Hotel to the A82. Cross the A82 to the lay-by and join the path which runs west along the banks of the River Coupall. If the river is in spate, there is no choice but to follow the path round to the bridge by the Lagangarbh. If the river is low enough, cross it earlier and head more directly west to the mouth of the corrie from the point where the river swings away to the north.

Both bothies passed on the route to the corrie are private. The first, a little way along the path, is the Jacksonville hut owned by the exclusive Creag Dhu club. The second, Lagangarbh, at the bottom of the path up Coire na Tulaich, is owned by the Scottish Mountaineering Club and is available for affiliated associations.

As you approach the corrie, its massive walls loom like a cathedral above you. Except after rain, when the hill's characteristic red hue shines through, the walls are an austere dark grey. Any route, let alone a straightforward one, to the ridge looks impossible. The closer you get to the corrie's mouth, however, the more reasonable the gradient becomes.

Much worse than the scramble in the summer is fighting off the midges. They hang around in clouds in the corrie, waiting to attack unsuspecting walkers sweating their way up the path or along the dried-up burn. An extra application of insect repellent before you start the ascent is advisable.

The path climbs steeply but comfortably up the right-hand side of the corrie. It crosses small rock outcrops and bouldery patches on its way to the scree slopes visible at the top. Despite the inhospitable nature of the corrie, a variety of different plants manage to cling to the rocks and crags. Small clumps of azalea, the ubiquitous yellow saxifrage, heather and a variety of mosses enliven the stony gloom. The steep zigzags of the Devil's Staircase, the start of tomorrow's walk, and the moor stretching off to the Blackwater Reservoir appear across Glen Coe behind you as you climb.

The most difficult section of the climb comes in the top third of the corrie. The path zigzags across steep scree slopes which give a slow and laborious route to the top. Those who prefer their rocks more solidly fixed to the ground can avoid most if not all of the scree by keeping to the right and picking a route over the rocks and small grassy slopes on a series of outcrops just below the ridge.

The ascent is quick – particularly if you are racing to escape the midges – and you should reach the ridge little more than an hour after entering the corrie. In wet or snowy conditions the going will be harder.

The col at the summit of the corrie is marked by a small cairn. The route up to Stob Dearg along the path which heads east from the col is also marked with cairns to help you find your way in poor visibility. Given the treacherously steep walls dropping off on each side of the route to the summit, the cairns are useful in mist or low cloud. The rockiness of the terrain on the way to the summit means the path is faint at best and disappears completely in places. Careful compass work is essential if conditions are bad.

The path zigzags across a boulderfield of loose granite rocks. The summit lies further away than you would think and is concealed at the end of the ridge beyond some deceptive false summits. Even so, it should take less than half an hour to reach the top from the col.

The view on a good day is extensive. Stob Dearg offers one of the best vantage-points for Rannoch

Buachaille Etive Mor from the River Coupall

Moor. The flat moorland, dotted with blue jewel-like lochs and pools, stretches eastwards for miles, bounded to the north by the Black Corries and to the south by Beinn an Dothaidh and the other Tyndrum hills. More arresting is the volcanic tower of Schiehallion at the edge of Loch Rannoch. Its position as the eastern marker of Rannoch Moor and its distinctive shape make it easier to identify than its southern neighbour Ben Lawers, although that mountain towers more than 130m above Schiehallion's 1,083m.

At the western edge of the moor is the Kings House Hotel, nestling toy-like more than 700m below. The summit gives a good perspective on the tortuous course of the River Coupall which encircles the Buachaille. The burn rises at the watershed high up the Lairig Gartain and flows north through the glen on the hill's west side. It turns east at Altnafeadh along the Buachaille's northern flank then curls south again to join the River Etive as it flows down to Loch Etive at the end of the glen.

The view of Rannoch Moor from the Buachaille is justly famous, but it is not the only attraction of the summit. Bidean nam Bian's peaks and corries dominate the western sky-line. The view emphasises how fickle Hugh Munro was in allowing only one Munro from the four 1,000m-plus peaks which make up the Bidean range.

The view of Bidean grows in splendour as you retrace your steps back down to the col. The massive bulk of Bidean and the peaks surrounding it confirm that, if Buachaille Etive Mor is forbidding, Glen Coe is positively intimidating. Although its history has made it one of the most famous glens in Scotland, it

Rannoch Moor from Buachaille Etive Mor

can sometimes seem the most desolate spot in the Highlands. The massive bulk of the Three Sisters juts out from Bidean's main peak, almost touching the precipitous wall of the Aonach Eagach as it looms over the bleak glen.

The National Trust, which now owns the glen, has recently decided to restore some of the natural forest which once covered much of its length. For now, however, there is scarcely a tree or bush to interrupt the desolation. Loch Achtriochtan at its western end is too small to soften the sheer granite walls of the glen, as Loch Leven does in the neighbouring glen in the north. The River Coe rushes quickly along its flat course as if its sole aim was to flee the 'Glen of Weeping' as quickly as possible.

Glen Coe is at its most forbidding in bad weather: grey storm clouds and battering rain seem ideally suited to its glowering mountains. Sunshine and soft light seem incongruous, serving only to emphasise, rather than lighten, its barrenness.

The landscape perfectly fits the glen's murderous history. For most people, Glen Coe is famous not for mountains but for the massacre of the MacDonald clan in February 1692. There were more brutal massacres and higher death tolls in other Highland skirmishes, but Glen Coe is remembered because the tradition of Highland hospitality was so brutally betrayed and because the massacre was at least tacitly approved by the king. That made it another chapter in the Scots' constant fight against the domination by the Auld Enemy, the English.

The origins of the massacre lie in the proposals to merge the Scottish and English parliaments. The two crowns had been joined almost 90 years before and, in some quarters of the Scottish establishment, pressure to complete the process with a merger of the two parliaments was growing. One of the main supporters of the union was Sir John Dalrymple, Master of Stair and King William's principal secretary of state for Scotland.

The biggest obstacle in persuading the king and the English parliament of the wisdom of taking full responsibility for Scotland was the wild and lawless Highland clans. The plan was to buy their loyalty but, although the clan chiefs were generally willing to take the money, King William was unwilling to put up the amounts required. Thanks to that, and deceit and greed in its administration, the scheme failed.

The next proposal was to offer a pardon to all rebels provided they signed an oath of allegiance to the king by 1 January 1692 with the threat of the 'utmost extremity of the law' to those who did not sign. Even as the clan chiefs were deliberating on whether or not to sign, Dalrymple was plotting ways of forcing them to comply by using 'all manner of hostility' on them, and particularly on his arch enemies, the MacDonalds of Glen Coe.

The excuse to put the plans into action was soon forthcoming. MacIain, chief of the Glen Coe Mac-Donalds, delayed his journey to sign the oath until the very last day, arriving in Fort William on 31 December. There, he was told that the oath could only be accepted by a civil magistrate, resident at Inveraray, so he was forced to race there. Delayed by a snowstorm, he did not reach Inveraray until 2 January and, because the magistrate was absent, did not finally swear allegiance until 6 January.

Plenty of other clan chiefs were late in signing but Dalrymple decided to make an example of the 'thieving tribe' of the Glen Coe MacDonalds. They had a long record of robbery, murder and rebellion. The poor conditions of their own glen forced them to make raids into neigbouring territories to steal cattle, often hiding them in the beautiful Coire Gabhail, the lost valley, between Beinn Fhada and Gearr Aonach on the south side of Glen Coe. Their actions had won them few friends among rival clans.

King William, preoccupied with a war with France, approved orders to 'extirpate that sept of thieves' – although whether he was actually aware of what he signed is a matter of debate. Dalrymple's plans were put into action. Two companies of the Earl of Argyll's regiment were selected, under the control of Captain Robert of Glenlyon. Although related to MacIain by marriage, Glenlyon had reason to hate the MacDonalds as a raid on his glen had tipped him into bankruptcy, forcing him into the regiment at the age of 60.

His troops took up lodgings with the people of Glen Coe on 1 February, the marital relationship ensuring they were hospitably received. Twelve days later, orders for the massacre were sent from Edinburgh and relayed to Lt-Col James Hamilton in Fort William. At 5 a.m. on 13 February Glenlyon gave orders to kill all men under 70. About 36 of MacIain's men were killed, including the chief himself, who died in his own bedroom. Three or four women and children were also slaughtered but most of the remaining clan, some 400 people, escaped into the hills, where many perished in blizzards.

It would be easy to blame the massacre for the emptiness today of Glen Coe but the death toll was relatively small, partly because some of the soldiers were not over-zealous in carrying out their orders. The MacDonalds in fact, quickly re-established themselves in their old settlements. The almost complete lack of human habitation between Kingshouse in the east and Glencoe village in the west today is a legacy of the Highland clearances, not of Dalrymple's murderous plot.

The glen was not always empty; indeed, at the end of the eighteenth century there was concern about over-population given the paucity of resources to support the glen's inhabitants, who lived by hunting, fishing and grazing traditional black cattle. They were driven out not by battles and skirmishes but by sheep or, more precisely, by profit-hungry land-owners.

The clearances started in the mid-eighteenth century and continued for 60 years, a slow and painful process of converting huge tracts of land to sheep-grazing. Some Highlanders were forcibly evicted, others were gradually squeezed out as the land available for grazing their cattle dwindled and the clan chiefs began to demand money for rent, instead of payments in kind. The attractions of sheep-farming were irresistible. The wool and mutton could be sold for high prices and tending a whole glen full of sheep required little more than the cost of a shepherd and his sheepdogs.

It is difficult to establish how much of the Highland population was forced out during the clearances. Some historians blame the clearances as much on over-population as on aggressive landlords. But today, 150 years later, there are plenty of signs of abandoned settlements and dwellings scattered on the hillsides. The clearances even had a dramatic impact on the landscape itself, as forests were chopped down to make way for sheep, then the sheep grazed on the shoots which might have regenerated the trees.

Like many other parts of the Highlands, the floor of Glen Coe was once covered by the Caledonian forest. The only remains are those few parts which have been fenced off from sheep. The emptiness of the glen will become increasingly apparent as you descend into the Lairig Gartain, the wide pass between the two 'Herdsmen of the Etive' – Buachaille Etive Mor and its smaller neighbour, Buachaille Etive Beag.

To continue the route after returning to the col from Stob Dearg, head west then south-west from the cairn at the top of Coire na Tulaich along the ridge towards the next of the Buachaille's peaks, Stob na Doire. If the weather is poor, you may prefer to drop directly back down through the corrie again.

For the route along the ridge a clear path climbs west first of all over an unnamed top, marked 902m on the OS map, then heads south-west. This gives the opportunity to admire the fine ridge of the Buachaille Etive Beag just across the Lairig Gartain, its shape uncannily similar to the Buachaille Etive Mor. Just before the ridge steepens towards the final ascent of Stob na Doire, the path drops down to the right to skirt a rocky outcrop. It is easier to head over the rocks as the path round them to the west is eroded and there is a steep drop to the Lairig Gartain below.

The ridge narrows, giving dramatic drops on both sides and particularly good views south into Coire Cloiche Finne. It widens again as the path climbs up rockier slopes to Stob na Doire's summit. From here you can see Loch Etive and the small artificial lake, Lochan Urr, above it. Glen Etive and its loch are among the most beautiful in Scotland and, because the road ends at the top of the loch, they are quiet and unspoilt. It is well worth a return trip to the area to visit the loch and climb some of the hills around it, including Ben Starav and Beinn Trilleachan.

To continue the excursion from the summit of Stob na Doire, go south-west down the path – beware of dropping directly south as that way lies a steep drop down to Glen Etive far below. The route zigzags down through rocks and boulders to the bealach between Stob na Doire and the next peak, Stob Coire Altrium. It is possible to carry on south-west over that top and on to the end of the ridge to admire the fine views of Loch Etive as it heads out to the Atlantic near Oban. You should nonetheless return to descend to the Lairig Gartain from this col, as the slopes from the ridge further along are steep and rocky and it is difficult to pick a safe way down.

The path down to the Lairig Gartain can be clearly seen on the right at the other side of the bealach. Cut across north-west to the path from the low point of the bealach to avoid the steeper, more eroded parts at the top. A faint track contours across the head of the corrie towards the main path from the low point of the bealach. The main path zigzags easily north down the slope into the Lairig Gartain.

About halfway down, where a couple of burns converge, the path steepens and becomes rocky and eroded. This section requires care, particularly in wet conditions when water flows over the rocks. It is only a short section and the slope becomes more gradual and the terrain grassier as you approach the floor of the glen.

The path through the Lairig Gartain runs along the north-western bank of the River Coupall, so cross the river at the end of the descent from the col and scramble up the steep bank on the other side. The wide, open floor of the Lairig, with its sides curving up to the cliffs at the top of the two Buachailles, is a perfect contrast to the cloistered climb up the steep Coire na Tulaich at the start of the day.

Less than an hour strolling through the glen brings you to the end of the path at the A82 road. Unfortunately, there is not a path along the river all the way back to Lagangarbh. Even in the driest conditions, picking a way through the peat hags and heather is irritating. It is better to suffer ten minutes of traffic and walk along the A82 road to Lagangarbh to pick up the path back to the Kings House Hotel. The path starts near the footbridge by Lagangarbh cottage and returns along the River Coupall.

The area of Glen Coe owned by the National Trust stretches from Altnafeadh to the Aonach Eagach above the Clachaig Inn and down Glen Etive to Dalness. The Dalness Forest, which includes the two Buachailles, was bought in 1937 with money raised under an initiative by the Scottish Mountaineering Club. The driving force behind the fundraising was Percy Unna, who subsequently bequeathed his fortune to the NTS for similar purposes. In his bequest to purchase Glen Coe he asked that 'the land should be maintained in its primitive condition for all time'. Purists complain that the National Trust breaches the terms of his legacy simply by maintaining paths and erecting signposts. As you stroll back along the path to Kingshouse, however, you should be grateful to enjoy the fruits of his generosity in one of Britain's few remaining wildernesses.

Stalking: National Trust for Scotland, no restrictions

Day 7

Kingshouse to Kinlochleven

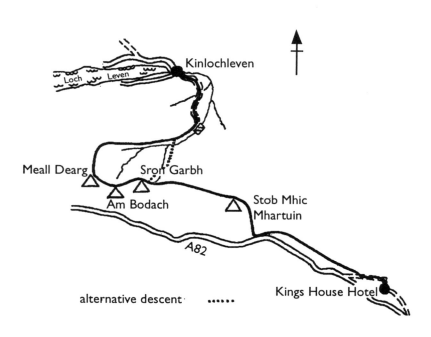

Kinlochleven

Loch Leven

Meall Dearg

Sron Garbh

Am Bodach

Stob Mhic Mhartuin

A82

Kings House Hotel

alternative descent ······

Day 7
Aonach Eagach

Kingshouse to Kinlochleven

ROUTE SUMMARY

Follow the route of the West Highland Way from the Kings House Hotel and climb the Devil's Staircase. From the top of the Staircase, go west along the ridge over Stob Mhic Mhartuin, Sron Garbh and Am Bodach to Meall Dearg. Descend north-west to the col between Meall Dearg and Garbh Bheinn. From the col turn east down the glen to join the track leading to Kinlochleven.

Distance: 20km
Time: 8hr
Ascent: 1,117m
Descent: 1,252m

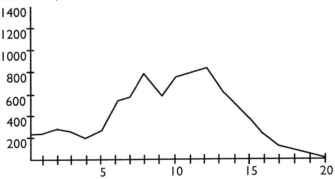

They knew what they were doing when they named Aonach Eagach. 'The Notched Ridge', towering more than 900m above Glen Coe, twists and climbs above gullies and across pinnacles as it winds its way for seven miles between the Devil's Staircase and the Pap of Glencoe. As a ridge walk, it is unparalleled on the British mainland. Although not the longest ridge, it is one of the narrowest. It gives heart-stopping glimpses down the yawning gullies which plunge into Glen Coe and, when you have the time to appreciate them, outstanding views across Bidean nam Bian to the south and the Mamores to the north.

Today's walk includes the most difficult section of the Highland High Way. The 23m descent from Am Bodach towards Meall Dearg involves scrambling down a near-vertical rock-face. Other parts of the ridge are rough and eroded as walkers' feet have added to the effects of the weather. It is a challenging traverse even in the best of conditions. But with care, experience of rough scrambling and a reasonable head for heights, it is achievable, if nerve-wracking at times.

The ridge should not be attempted in winter except by climbers experienced in such conditions. Snow and ice make an already narrow ridge treacherous to the inexperienced. Add the effects of the wind, which whistles through the gaps in the ridge with fearsome force, and it can defeat even the most accomplished of winter climbers. Ropes, crampons and ice-axes, and skill in using them, are essential. For such conditions, an alternative descent into Kinlochleven drops down from the ridge just before it reaches Sron Garbh. Those who are not confident of their ability to negotiate steep cliffs and narrow ridges should use this alternative in other seasons too.

The Highland High Way traverses about half of the Aonach Eagach dropping north to Kinlochleven from Meall Dearg, the first of only two Munros on the ridge. It misses out the Crazy Pinnacles – a good thing or bad thing depending on whether you suffer from vertigo or enjoy airy scrambling. The section between Am Bodach and Meall Dearg, called The Chancellor, is crazy enough for most tastes.

The descent into Kinlochleven is far easier than any of the routes back to Glen Coe. Almost all the routes south involve scrambling down steep, eroded and dangerous slopes. The route north from Meall Dearg, by contrast, is a short scramble then an easy stroll through the Mhorair glen which lies between the Aonach Eagach and Garbh Bheinn.

Should you wish to walk the full length of the ridge, it is still possible to avoid the difficult descent into Glen Coe by continuing to the Pap of Glencoe, Sgorr na Ciche, then descending north. Although officially the end of the Aonach Eagach, the Pap is often left out by those who traverse the ridge, so missing the splendid views from its summit. From the summit there is a route down its north-eastern flank to Caolasnacon, on the road along the south side of Loch Leven. From there Gaelic Bus operates an early-evening service to Kinlochleven.

The Highland High Way starts the traverse at the most easterly point of the Aonach Eagach on top of the Devil's Staircase, instead of the more conventional starting point at the foot of Am Bodach further west in Glen Coe. The early part of the ridge is broad and grassy and the walking easy, giving plenty of time to enjoy the views of the more challenging terrain to come.

To reach the Devil's Staircase, follow the West Highland Way markers from the Kings House Hotel west along the military road for three miles to Altnafeadh. From there, the Devil's Staircase climbs north, marked by a finger-signpost pointing the way to Kinlochleven. Part of the old military road to Fort William, the Devil's Staircase was built around 1750. It was christened by the 450 men from the Rich's and Guise's regiments involved in its construction, in recognition of the difficulty in laying it rather than the effort of climbing it. While it has been improved and maintained by the West Highland Way rangers, the skill of the original construction is still evident in the drainage channels and kerbing as it zigzags up the side of the hill. Its well-preserved state also owes much to its being replaced, about 35 years after its construction, by a new military road. That took the

The Blackwater Reservoir from the Devil's Staircase

less direct but lower route now followed by the A82 through Glen Coe and Ballachulish to Fort William. The Devil's Staircase forms one stage in the Scottish Six Days motorbike trials, held in early summer – a time to be avoided by walkers.

Climbing the Devil's Staircase gives widening views back over the Buachaille Etive Mor, particularly rewarding for those who tackled it yesterday on the excursion from the route. There are also splendid perspectives of Black Mount and through the sweep of the Lairig Gartain between the two Buachailles.

The top of the Devil's Staircase is marked by two large cairns. A clear path from these leads west to the ridge, climbing gradually towards Stob Mhic Mhartuin. This small top is a good place to stop for breakfast or an early-morning snack and enjoy the excellent views of the south side of Glen Coe and across Rannoch Moor. From this vantage-point you can also pick out the peaks of the Mamore ridge, climbed on the next stage of the route and the third excursion from the Highland High Way. The cone of Binnein Beag is the most distinctive hill in the Mamores, standing slightly apart from the main ridge at its eastern end. Towards the western edge is Stob Ban, distinguished by a quartzite cap which can look like snow, the most impressive of the three summits on the final day of the route into Glen Nevis.

Having enjoyed the view from Stob Mhic Mhartuin, head west up the grassy banks then turn north-west to gain the ridge. Take care in poor visibility not to continue too far west after Stob Mhic Mhartuin or you could begin to descend back into Glen Coe. Once on the ridge, a faint path winds

Stob Mhic Mhartuin is a good place to rest

south-west then west as it passes Sron a'Choire Odhair-Bhig. The north-eastern ridge from this summit makes an easy walk down to join the West Highland Way path into Kinlochleven should weather conditions necessitate a change of plan. The Highland High Way continues west along the ridge to the unnamed top, marked 903m on the OS map.

From the unnamed summit you will get your first glimpse of Kinlochleven, today's destination, nestling below the steep slopes of the Mamores in the north. Already you will be able to pick out the distinctive white building of the Mamores Lodge, whose commanding position above the town makes it visible from miles around. There are steep drops off to the right but the ridge is still broad enough to give easy walking.

From the unnamed top head south-west, keeping close to the right-hand edge to avoid straying south into Glen Coe. The point at which the ridge changes direction to head north-west to Sron Garbh is marked by a small cairn on a black rock. Just south of this point is a prominent outcrop called A' Chailleach, 'the old woman', companion to 'the old man', Am Bodach, facing it across the corrie. It is a leisurely stroll from here along spongy grass to Sron Garbh's rocky crest.

Those who prefer not to tackle the Aonach Eagach can go north into Kinlochleven just before the ridge climbs to Sron Garbh. The best place to drop off the ridge is at the low point of the col between the cairn that marks the change of direction and Sron Garbh. Descend just before the two rocky outcrops, separated by a grass strip. The initial descent is steep but not difficult, and it quickly broadens out to a wide grassy bank. Drop gradually to the burn and cross it when possible. On the east side there are broken paths and sheep tracks which make the descent easier. If the burn is in spate make the crossing as high up as possible to avoid being trapped on the west side.

Numerous gullies, created by the burns which run down from the ridge on the right of the corrie, make the going tiresome. Keeping close to the side of the burn saves the effort of bobbing up and down through the gullies, but the ground here is wetter. Lower down the glen, you will pick up sheep tracks a little way above the burn which make the going easier.

When you reach the floor of the glen between Garbh Bheinn and the Aonach Eagach, turn right and head north-east to Kinlochleven. If Feith nan Lab, the burn running through the glen, is in spate, continue on its right side to the small reservoir where you pick up the path into Kinlochleven. If the burn is low enough, cross to the left side of the burn to use the tracks across the flood plain which take you down to the route of the Highland High Way. Carry on along the edge of the burn to the reservoir.

To continue along the Aonach Eagach, climb the ridge to the summit of Sron Garbh. The rock turns from the pinkish-red granite, the predominent rock on the Buachaille and some of Black Mount, to the green-grey Dalradian strata which characterise the next part of the ridge.

The hills of Glen Coe are an island of igneous rock, the remains of a succession of lava flows which poured from the earth's core more than 300 million years ago. Most such lavas were long ago swept away by glaciers and erosion, but the Glen Coe hills survived. They are the remains of a ring fault measuring about 14km by 8km which sank into a cauldron of molten lava and were baked to an impervious granite. The upper layers of softer lava were gradually stripped away, exposing the resistant rhyolite which gives the area its formidable cliffs and buttresses.

The distinct layers of rock are clearly marked on the face of Gearr Aonach, the middle of the Three Sisters which glower down on the south side of Glen Coe. While the top third is lighter, acidic rhyolite, the lower two-thirds are darker andesite. Evidence of the force of the Ice Age is equally clear in the crags, corries and ridges which give Glen Coe such a variety of walking and climbing terrain.

Erosion and weathering continue today. Large chunks of rock occasionally tumble down into Glen Coe. In 1980 the road through it was blocked after heavy rain caused a rapid thaw which brought down large boulders from the summit of the Aonach Eagach to Achtriochtan.

From the stony summit of Sron Garbh the ridge continues south-west towards Am Bodach. The path becomes clearer as it is joined by the route up from Glen Coe, the more common approach to the Aonach Eagach. As you approach Am Bodach you get the first view of The Chancellor dipping and twisting west from its summit. The views become more spectacular the closer you get. Even those who decide against tackling the ridge should climb Am Bodach to appreciate what they are missing. The scramble is easier than it looks from the approach and the views down into Glen Coe and along the ridge make it worth the effort.

The Chancellor is known locally as Ptarmigan Ridge because so many of those birds are found on it. They are recognised by their ungainly movements and you may spot one blundering to get out of your way. The distinctive whistle of the golden plover is also a frequent accompaniment as you crawl tentatively along the ridge from Am Bodach.

Scramble up Am Bodach's rocky face to the summit cairn. From there the path continues west and then appears to come to a dead stop. The next 30 minutes are the most difficult of the entire Highland High Way. The west side of the summit is a precipitous cliff which plunges first to the ridge and then into the glen far below. It is difficult to believe there is any way down, let alone one accessible to walkers. But, as the Scottish Mountaineering Club guide says, with suitably vague understatement, 'a cast to the right should succeed'. The crags are steep and the going precarious but there are enough foot-

The descent from Am Bodach to The Chancellor

and handholds to give a steady, careful way down the 23m drop to the more secure terrain of the ridge proper. As the SMC guide suggests, the descent is best tackled from the right-hand side of the summit plateau until about halfway down to the ridge. There the ground flattens slightly and the rocks ahead present what seems an impossible cliff. Instead of trying to navigate it, take the easier route on the south of the rocks. Go through a small gap on the left just as the ground flattens. That brings you round to the Glen Coe side of the ridge. Descend by clambering down a series of oversized steps. The start of The Chancellor proper is marked by a fence post at the top of a deep gully plunging down into Glen Coe.

Having struggled this far, you may question the arbitrary way in which Sir Hugh Munro decided what constituted a Munro and what a subsidiary peak. An easy stroll between Ben Oss and Ben Dubhchraig, or Beinn Dorain and Beinn an Dothaidh, brings two Munros. Despite the long walk up and difficult scramble down, Am Bodach merits only a top; the Munro lies half a mile ahead on Meall Dearg.

The worst scrambling of the day is now over, although traversing the rest of the ridge to the Munro still requires care. The ridge broadens after it passes a large cairn, descends a little then climbs again to the large rounded plateau which tops Meall Dearg.

Meall Dearg has a key place in Munro-bagging history. It was the last one climbed by the Revd A.E. Robertson, the first person to climb all the Munros. To help him celebrate his achievement, he invited his wife and his best friend to accompany him on his final Munro. The friend records that, in true mountaineer style, he marked the occasion by kissing first the summit cairn, then his wife.

From Meall Dearg, the ridge stretches ahead across the Crazy Pinnacles towards the next Munro of Sgorr Nam Fiannaidh. The Highland High Way takes a much less daunting route down Meall Dearg's northern shoulder. Just north of the summit cairn is a large creamy white boulder. It is an erratic boulder deposited there by a glacier, further evidence of the effect of the Ice Age on the local area.

The descent from Meall Dearg is a boulderfield strewn with hunks of pink porphyrite. The ridge is steep in parts and care is needed to avoid straying on to the rocky outcrop. Head slightly east of north to the watershed between Allt Gleann a' Chaolais in the west and Feith nan Lab – unnamed on the OS map – in the east. From there go east through the glen, following the line of the Feith nan Lab but keeping about 200m above it on the left. This keeps you out of the worst bogs and you will pick up a path, albeit broken and indistinct, which winds down through the glen.

From the northern slopes of Meall Dearg, Loch Leven looks more like a river than a loch. The slender section at Caolasnacon, which translates as 'narrows of Con', was a problem before the road along from Glencoe village was completed in 1922. Until then, supplies from the south were brought in by boat along the loch. The narrowest part of the loch was not permanently cleared until 1907 and the Chaolais burn had to be diverted to prevent it blocking up the narrows with more silt. Until the dredging was accomplished, only empty boats could be sure of getting through on certain tides. If the water was too low, passengers had to get out of the boat and walk around the narrow stretches. Cars replaced boats as a way of getting to Kinlochleven when the road along the south side of the loch was

Looking along the Aonach Eagach

completed in 1922. It was started using prisoner-of-war labour from the First World War, and is still known locally as the German Road.

Garbh Bheinn, which lies between here and the loch, is a fearsome-looking hill from any angle. The inhabitants of Kinlochbeg, as the southern end of Kinlochleven is officially called, have just cause to resent it; so close and steep are its sides that the sun does not rise above it for three months in the winter so the houses at its foot are shrouded in gloom until spring.

Garbh Bheinn was the spot chosen by Robert Louis Stevenson as the hiding-place for Alan Breck and David Balfour, the heroes of his famous novel, *Kidnapped.* The book is his fictional account of the true story of the murder of Colin Campbell of Glenure, one of the agents appointed by the king to administer the lands seized from the rebel clans after the defeat of the Jacobites at Culloden. Glenure would have been doubly unpopular as the Campbells were one of the few clans not to back the Jacobite cause. In the book, Breck creeps down to Caolasnacon to pick up food for himself and Balfour and to leave a message asking for funds from James Stewart, his friend and protector. In real life, James was blamed for Campbell's murder and hanged on the knoll just above the Ballachulish ferry at the head of Loch Leven. It is believed that the Campbells knew who murdered their kinsman but, for political reasons, allowed an innocent man to die. The elders of Clan Campbell are said still to pass on the true identity of the Appin murderer from one generation to another. Stewart's corpse was chained to the gibbet so that it could not be stolen and given a decent burial before the flesh had rotted and the bones had been picked clean by birds of prey and foxes.

The descent to Kinlochleven continues along the side of Garbh Bheinn getting closer to the burn as it passes through a small gorge at the end of the high plateau. Views back towards The Chancellor are spectacular, the distance accentuating its narrowness and steep drops.

After you pass the gorge, the vegetation changes. The slopes become green and grassy, sprinkled with ferns and small mountain plants including saxifrage, milkwort and campion in spring and summer. The ground becomes very wet after rain. Keeping above the floor of the glen gives the driest walking.

At a dam near the mouth of the glen the burn widens to a large pool lined with birch and rowan trees. A little below this, a bridge crosses the burn where the route continues along the track down into Kinlochleven.

Kinlochleven was almost renamed Aluminiumville at the turn of the century and the reason becomes obvious as you follow the track into the town. First come a series of huge pipes descending the hill, then the sheds of the aluminium smelter come into view. The factory is the reason Kinlochleven remains one of the Highland's main population centres, despite being bypassed by the Balluchulish bridge since it opened in 1975. The town has a supermarket, a baker, newsagent and general store as well as a bank – albeit one only open on Thursdays. Before the bridge was built, the town attracted tourists who preferred the leisurely drive round the loch to the long queue for the ferry, or who had heard of the beauty of Loch Leven. The bridge cut the number of tourists dramatically. The industry, too, will soon all but disappear.

The smelter was built by the British Aluminium Company, now British Alcan, and employed 1,000 people when it opened in 1907. It is the oldest and smallest smelter in the world. Its technology is outdated, its products too specialised and its markets far away. By 1995 it employed less than 100 people and British Alcan has made it clear that it will eventually close, although no date has been set. The company does intend to keep the power station, a listed building, using the electricity to power its other smelter in Lochaber or to sell to the National Grid.

To those visiting the town today, it may seem surprising that the smelter has lasted so long. It is many miles from the nearest town, never mind any port or station. The cost of bringing in raw materials and transporting the aluminium back out again must make the economics of smelting here questionable at best. The advantages of manufacturing in a larger, more modern plant easily outweigh the attractions of Kinlochleven's particularly pure product.

At the start of the century, however, such considerations were less important than the abundance of water and the means with which to turn it into power. Annual rainfall of 104cm made it a perfect place to build a power station. The British Aluminium Company bought the Blackwater glen in the mid-1890s, relocating the few people who lived there, and constructed one of the country's largest dams.

The dam took four years to build and employed 3,000 men. It is almost a kilometre long, 25m high and holds back water diverted to the reservoir in rivers and feeder dams from 65 square miles around. It was the last great project of the true navvies, the reckless, feckless hard-drinking men who built the canals and railways of Britain. An evocative account of the life of a dam-worker in *Children of the Dead End* by Patrick MacGill brings to life the harsh existence on the site and the spirit of those who built the dam.

MacGill worked as a navvy on the site and he recounts how one day they were collecting a shilling (5p) from each man in the gang in order to send a sick colleague home to Skye to die. The next day they were playing cards for the collection as the poor man had died in the night before he could make the journey.

The men worked 10-hour shifts, living in spartan conditions. Teams of five did the drilling, four striking the drill with sledgehammers which the fifth held between his knees. Those who wanted a drink had to walk across the Devil's Staircase to Kingshouse. The bodies of some who risked the journey in winter were found months later, when the snows had melted. A small graveyard – which contains one headstone with the inscription 'Not Known' – near the dam bears testament to some of those who died during the construction work.

The Mamore Lodge is now a comfortable hotel, one of three in the town. Kinlochleven also boasts two bunkhouses, one of them at the Mamore Lodge and the other in the town, as well as numerous bed & breakfasts and a couple of campsites. It offers the first shop since Tyndrum, as well as a pub with a jukebox and pool table.

While considerable efforts are being made to stimulate tourism and other sources of employment, the area's success in maintaining its inhabitants when the smelter is closed remains to be seen. It could be that the town which grew with the smelter will die with its departure. For now, it provides an excellent place to end a dramatic day on the Highland High Way.

USEFUL INFORMATION

Accommodation: MacDonald Hotel,
    01855 831539
  Tail Race Inn, 01855 831402
  Mamore Lodge Hotel, 01855 831213
  Elsie Robertson, Edencoille, Garbhenn Road
    01855 831358
  Miss McAngus, Hermon, Rob Roy Road,
    01855 831383
  Mr and Mrs Napier, Tigh-Na-Cheo, 01855
    831434
  Mrs F. MacLean, Quiraing, 43 Lovat Road,
    01855 831580
Bunkhouses: West Highland Lodge, 01855 831471
Mamore Lodge Hotel, 01855 831213
Camping: Macdonald Hotel, 01855 831539
Transport: Gaelic bus from Fort William,
    01855 811229
Supplies: Various shops, restaurants and a post
  office in village
Bank: Royal Bank of Scotland, open Thursday
Stalking: National Trust, no restrictions
Tourist Information: Fort William, 01397 703781

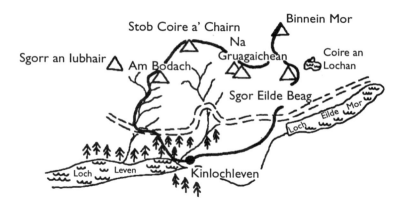

Sgorr an Iubhair

Stob Coire a' Chairn

Na Gruagaichean

Binnein Mor

Coire an Lochan

Am Bodach

Sgor Eilde Beag

Loch Eilde Mor

Loch Leven

Kinlochleven

Excursion 3

The Mamores

Excursion 3
The Mamores

ROUTE SUMMARY

From the carpark near the falls in Kinlochleven, climb the path north-east to Sgor Eilde Beag. On the ridge go north-west to the unnamed summit, at 1,062m, and on to Binnein Mor. Return to the unnamed top and go west along the ridge to Na Gruagaichean, Stob Coire a' Chairn and Am Bodach. Continue west to the col before Sgorr an Iubhair. Turn south off the ridge to the vehicle track. Return to Kinlochleven on the West Highland Way.

Distance: 19km
Time: 9hr 30min
Ascent: 1,592m
Descent: 1,592m

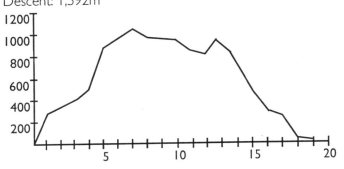

For an area which boasts eleven Munros, seven tops and one of the finest ridge-walks in Britain, the Mamores are an underrated set of hills. On a clear day Glen Coe and Ben Nevis can seem busier than Sauchiehall Street on a Saturday afternoon as hordes of climbers and walkers swarm over the ridges and summits. The Mamores, by contrast, seem like a haven of tranquillity and have some of the best walking in Scotland.

True, the Mamores do not have the narrow arêtes and brooding rock-faces of Glen Coe, nor can they boast Britain's highest mountain among their peaks. What they do have, though, are some splendid hills – Stob Ban and Binnein Mor are two of the most attractive peaks on the Highland High Way – and a varied and exhilarating ridge-walk which stretches for ten miles. The hills are easily accessible on a network of stalkers' paths, making the climb up to the range far easier than the height and the steepness of the slopes would suggest.

To spend a day in the Mamores is to feel as if you have a foot in two worlds. On one side is the glittering jewel of Loch Leven, with the craggy peaks of Glencoe beyond. Away to the north is the classic Highland beauty of Glen Nevis, the perfect foil to the awesome bulk of Ben Nevis, and the Aonachs. Each twist of the ridge brings fresh perspectives on the other peaks in the range itself.

Bordered by Loch Leven in the south and Glen Nevis in the north, the Mamores cover an area of about 30 square miles between the two glens. Nestling deep at the end of the glacial valley, few of the summits can be seen from Kinlochleven; from there, the overwhelming impression is of the steepness of the slopes. As you will have appreciated from Buachaille Etive Mor and Aonach Eagach, the views from the south are enticing. The views from the north – and particularly from Carn Mor Dearg and its arête – are better still, especially in the early morning before the sun gets too high. But the best way to appreciate the contrast between the lofty ridges and the deep wide glens is by climbing the hills.

Mamore means 'moor of great size'. The reference to its size may be accurate, but the word moor seems entirely inappropriate to convey the peaks and corries, ridges and glens in the range. It is also called a forest in reference not to trees but to deer. The Mamore Forest is one of many hunting forests in Scotland, the name derived from the Latin term for 'an area outside an enclosure where hunting was permitted'. Herds of deer can be seen in the hills, particularly in spring or late autumn when they come down from the high tops.

All but two of the area's 11 Munros stand along a single ridge and its two northern spurs. The main ridge goes from Binnein Mor in the east to Mullach nan Coirean in the west. The two spurs branch into Glen Nevis and include the spectacular Devil's Ridge which crosses Sgurr a' Mhaim.

The really energetic can tick off all 11 Munros in the course of one long day but it is better to take time to savour their delights in a series of walks. Today's excursion and tomorrow's route into Fort William cover the seven Munros on the main ridge, leaving the two northern ridges and the eastern peaks of Binnein Beag and Sgurr Eilde Mor for later trips. Today includes the highest of the Mamores (Binnein

Heading up to the Mamore ridge

Mor) and the most dramatic (Na Gruagaichean) as well as the fine peaks of Stob Coire a' Chairn and the Highland High Way's second Am Bodach – the final, and most difficult, ascent of the day.

The four hills are close together but climbing them all makes it a full day. In total, today's excursion covers 13 map miles but the amount of climbing involved means it takes longer than that distance would suggest. There are a number of ways to shorten the day. The walking is very pleasant with only a little rough scrambling, particularly on the final climb to Am Bodach. The ridge does get quite narrow in places and can feel exposed in windy conditions. But at its lowest point it is still 745m high and, although the ridge does rise and fall, there is little extra climbing once you reach Sgor Eilde Beag.

The Mamores excursion begins on one of the many stalkers' paths which lead out of Kinlochleven. From the north side of the town follow the signs for the Grey Mare's Tail Waterfall to a carpark just behind the main street. Choose the left-hand (or highest) fork when the path from the carpark divides into three, and then branch right past some picnic tables when the path divides again.

The left-hand fork leads to the Grey Mare's Tail Waterfall named, with great originality, by Edward VII after his horse's tail. He stayed at the Mamore Lodge as a guest of the shipping magnate Frank Bibby when it was one of the great Scottish hunting estates. A five-minute detour will take you to the viewing platform for the falls, although its height and the deep gully which conceals its top means that only the noise gives a sense of its size and power.

A few minutes after passing the picnic tables take the path across the burn and follow it up the hill as it rises steeply east through a delightful wood of birch, beech and rowan trees, carpeted with bluebells in the late spring. You will be accompanied by the sound of numerous small waterfalls in the burns which border the path on both sides.

After 20 minutes of walking up eroded zigzags, the path leaves the forest. Behind you lie the Pap of

Glencoe and Mam na Gualainn, looking like twin beacons enticing visitors to enjoy the beauty of Loch Leven. Across to the south-west is a good view of yesterday's route along the Aonach Eagach.

The hills which lie ahead on today's route come into view as you leave the forest. The first peak, Binnein Mor, remains hidden until you reach the top of Sgor Eilde Beag, but you should be able to pick out the steep crown of Am Bodach at the head of the deeply dug Coire na Ba off to the north. Before long, Na Gruagaichean and Stob Coire a' Chairn, the second and third of the peaks, join it. These views are appetisers for the more dramatic perspectives from the ridge itself.

Continue up the path as it climbs through heather and peat hags round the north-western side of Meall an Doire Dharaich. A large cairn marks the point where the path meets the landrover track going from the Mamore Lodge to Loch Eilde Mor. Cross the track and continue along the smaller path which carries on, heading north-east across the moor round the steep, dark flank of Sgor Eilde Beag.

The network of stalkers' paths reflect the Mamores' hunting history. The estate's wealthy owners could afford large armies of servants to cut paths out of the hills in order to get deerstalkers up and ponies back down with the kill. It is a testament to the efforts of the original estate workers that the paths are still in such good condition, despite little maintenance, with only limited erosion or deterioration into bog.

The whole Mamore estate, and much of Ben Nevis, the Aonachs and the Grey Corries, is now owned by British Alcan, operator of the aluminium smelters in Kinlochleven and Lochaber on the outskirts of Fort William. It progressively bought up large tracts of land following its initial purchase for the Blackwater Reservoir in the 1890s, partly to enable it to divert water to feed the Kinlochleven power station and a similar station supplying power for its Lochaber factory. It is a benign owner, imposing few restrictions on access save a request to keep to recognised routes during the stalking season. Although British Alcan has said the Kinlochleven smelter will close eventually, the Lochaber plant looks safe – subject to the vagaries of the international aluminium market – following an investment programme in the mid-1990s which made it one of the most modern and efficient plants in the world. It also intends to keep both power stations so the Mamores seem likely to have a Canadian corporate landlord for some time to come.

The route climbs steadily north-east on a clear path, crossing a number of the burns which flow down the sides of Sgor Eilde Beag. Some of these – particularly the main burn, Allt Coire nan Laogh, not named on the OS map – can be tricky to cross after heavy rain, but a short detour upstream should give a route across. As you wind round the hill, Loch Eilde Mor comes into view off to the right, a glorious sight on a sunny day.

Forty-five minutes after crossing the landrover track, turn left on a path which zigzags steeply up Sgor Eilde Beag. Follow it to the start of the ridge at the summit of Sgor Eilde Beag – appropriately named 'little peak of the hind', given the number of deer in the area. It is possible to detour across to bag its larger sister, the confusingly spelt Sgurr Eilde

Mor, off to the east above Coire an Lochain. The normal approach is to climb the south-west ridge, which starts at the south-eastern corner of the lochan. The slope is steep and the terrain rocky, so it will take over two hours to get to the summit and back to the route of the excursion.

The well-laid path zigzags steeply up to Sgor Eilde Beag, ending at the summit. This path is not marked on the OS map but, like most of the other Mamore stalking paths, it has been extended to the top of the hill by the passage of thousands of pairs of feet. Stalkers may not have wanted to get to the tops of hills as deer are never seen on summits; Munro-baggers and walkers most certainly do.

The summit of Sgor Eilde Beag marks the end of the longest climb of the day, although spurts of effort will be required for each of the four peaks to come. The route continues north-west along the edge of the steep Coire an Lochain, where there can be wide cornices in winter, to the unnamed top, marked 1,062m on the OS map. The path comes and goes but the walking is easy. Scrubby grass alternates with the broken quartz characteristic of most of the Mamore peaks.

A cairn on the unnamed peak marks the starting point for the short detour north to Binnein Mor. The path to it lies north along a short, narrow ridge. The closer you get to it, the more apparent is Binnein Mor's classic mountain shape, with its angular summit ridge and steep corries. Surprisingly, despite its shape and status as the highest of the Mamores, it is not one of the most notable features of the range from a distance. That accolade goes to its smaller sister, Binnein Beag, whose conical shape makes it instantly recognisable when viewed from the south, or to the sharp quartzite crest edges of Sgurr a' Mhaim and Stob Ban, which are most identifiable from Glen Nevis and the hills to the north.

As a viewpoint, however, Binnein Mor is unparalleled in the range. It offers an excellent platform for admiring the rest of the Mamore ridge. The two spurs containing An Gearanach and Sgurr a' Mhaim look at their best from here. Binnein Mor's easterly position also gives it a splendid perspective on the Grey Corries in the north and the peaks of the Glencoe and Black Mount hills, and Beinn Dorain and Beinn an Dothaidh and beyond in the south. Off to the south-east, the volcanic cone of Schiehallion marks the end of Rannoch's Moor's wilderness.

Four ridges fall away from the summit. The steep drops in the corries between them mean that on this hill you really do feel on top of the world. It is well worth the 40 or so minutes it will take you to get to the summit and back to the cairn where you rejoin the main ridge. Retrace your steps down the rocks surrounding its top and back along the ridge. There are steep drops west into Coire an Easain and east into Coire a' Bheinnin. Care is needed on the narrower sections, particularly during winter or in high winds.

From the unnamed top, the route continues south-west along the ridge to Na Gruagaichean. None of the views from the valley or the hills to the south quite prepare you for the remarkable symmetry of The Maidens' twin peaks. The dramatic U-shaped curve between them makes this one of the route's most memorable views.

The first of the Maidens' peaks is the higher, and

The Maidens, Na Gruagaichean

there is a steepish pull up to it from the ridge. More irritating is the 70m descent to the col between it and its sister peak. The path is severely eroded, particularly at the bottom where it is worn to loose earth. In wet or icy conditions this is especially treacherous. Care is needed in the selection of the route; slightly west of north is likely to give the best going.

From the col, a path heads left round the rock-face of the second top. The path becomes very eroded as it climbs back up to the ridge and it is best to carry on past the path a little way before scrambling up to the ridge again. If you look back you will see evidence of the change in geology which has produced the eroded paths, with the quartzite of Na Gruagaichean's summit giving way to softer rocks which wear more easily.

The more porous rocks also support more vegetation, as is obvious after the second of The Maidens' peaks. The boulders and rocks which littered the first narrow part of the ridge give way to broader, grassy slopes as it heads north-west. The lowest point on the ridge is marked by a couple of cairns identifying the start of a path dropping down into Coire na Ba and along a landrover track to the Mamore Lodge and Kinlochleven. Those who feel two summits are enough for the day can descend from the ridge here.

The long climb up to Stob Coire a' Chairn is an easy walk along a clear path, giving the chance to imagine the ancient glacial movements which carved out the broad, deep glens seen all around and which left the sharp ridges which make this such an enjoyable walk. While the long glens, like Glen Nevis, clearly mark the passage of ice sheets across the land, the corries in this and other ranges were the product of smaller, more localised glaciers. Where two of these met, they pressed out ridges and arêtes.

The sharpness of Binnein Mor, Stob Ban and Sgurr a' Mhaim reflects their quartzite rock, which was ground into jagged peaks by glacial action. The quartz is particularly noticeable on the latter two summits, making them look snow-covered in certain lights. The presence of quartzite in the region is even more evident in the Grey Corries north across Glen Nevis, whose pale-coloured crests gave the range its name.

Stob Coire a' Chairn marks the third Munro on the lazy S-shape which the ridge has taken to this point. It also gives the first clear view of the hills on tomorrow's route into Fort William. Stob Ban is already marked out as one of the stars of the Mamores, the steep sides of its magnificent corrie looking like sheer walls encircled by the protective arms of the ridge.

Stob Coire a' Chairn is the social centre of the Mamores, the crossroads for a variety of routes. To get here, walkers may have climbed up from Glen Nevis via An Garbhanach and An Gearanach, or be about to climb down to them having already bagged Sgurr a' Mhaim or Binnein Mor. They may have come up from Kinlochleven via Coire na Ba or Am Bodach and be about to complete the circle – enough to give plenty to talk about as you munch your sandwich and admire the splendid views.

Dedicated Munro-baggers will be tempted to head along the ridge to pick off An Gearanach. It is not a quick detour, however. An Gearanach is the second of the two tops and, although there is a clear path north, the ridge is narrow and steep in places so the traverse requires considerable care. The detour will add two hours to an already long day.

From Stob Coire a' Chairn, descend to Am Bodach across an unnamed top. The ridge narrows to produce an exhilarating walk, with fine views into the long, rolling glens on either side – Coire na Ba to the south and Coire a Mhail in the north – and across to Sgurr a' Mhaim on the Devil's Ridge. These overshadow the prospect of Ben Nevis's massive bulk, but no matter; the best views of it have been reserved for tomorrow.

The route up the apparently sheer face of Am Bodach is identified by a red line, marking the erosion of the path. From this angle, ascent may look well-nigh impossible. The route certainly is steep – possibly the steepest on the Highland High Way – but it is short: 30 minutes' climbing should easily get you to the top. While in places the slope is almost vertical, there are plenty of foot- and

The route up Am Bodach

handholds to help keep your balance. Keeping to the right of the gully will avoid the worst eroded sections.

On the plus side, the steep scramble gets you right to the summit cairn, where the views along the rest of the ridge are good enough to take your mind off your racing heart. The descent is much easier than the climb up. From the summit, the path continues west along the ridge across a boulderfield towards the next peak, Sgorr an Iubhair, which will be the first of tomorrow's hills. The boulders gradually give way to grassier slopes just at the low point of the ridge where a path leaves it to go south towards Kinlochleven.

Two cairns, one on the ridge path itself and the other slightly to the left, mark the start of the path down into Coire na h-Eirghe, which joins the track from Kinlochleven to Fort William through the Lairigmor. It will seem like a long walk along the ridge to pick up the path but it is faster than heading off across country in the hope of joining the path further down the corrie.

The clear path down Coire na h-Eirghe is an easy descent. The only possible difficulty is to identify the spot, about 30 minutes into the descent, where the path crosses to the right-hand side of the burn. The route is confusing here, but the best place to cross is where the burn levels out, about 200m, above a large prominent rock which stands on a plinth on the right-hand side of the burn. The path on the right side of the corrie is clear from here. Another sizeable burn, coming directly from Am Bodach, joins the main flow near the crossing spot. If you stay too long on the left-hand side of the burn the path peters out and it is easier to retrace your steps, at least part of the way, to cross the burn rather than to try to pick your way through the heather and bog on the east side.

As the route descends there are excellent views down to Loch Leven and across to the Aonach Eagach. Where the path reaches the landrover track, turn left over the metal bridge which crosses the burn you have followed down.

Those staying at the Mamore Lodge or its bunkhouse can continue east along the landrover track. Otherwise, return to Kinlochleven via the West Highland Way, which drops off to the right about ten minutes after the bridge. It descends through a pretty forest to reach the town on the north side of the loch, opposite the school.

Stalking: British Alcan Aluminium, 01397 702433

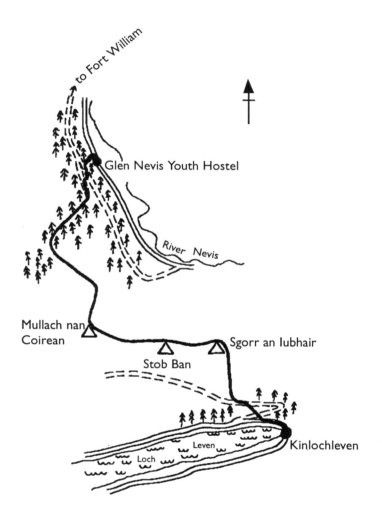

to Fort William

Glen Nevis Youth Hostel

River Nevis

Mullach nan Coirean

Stob Ban

Sgorr an Iubhair

Leven

Loch

Kinlochleven

Day 8

Kinlochleven
to Glen Nevis

Day 8
Stob Ban

Kinlochleven to Glen Nevis

ROUTE SUMMARY

Follow the West Highland Way from Kinlochleven then climb to the ridge between Am Bodach and Sgorr an Iubhair. Follow the ridge west over Sgorr an Iubhair and Stob Ban to Mullach nan Coirean. Descend the north ridge of Mullach nan Coirean then turn north-west to join the West Highland Way between two forest plantations. Follow the path into Glen Nevis and on to Fort William.

Distance: 19km
Time: 8hr 30min
Ascent: 1,696m
Descent: 1,686m

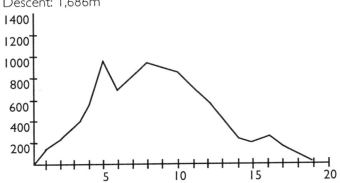

Today's route has a touch of finality about it. You can still enjoy one more day's walking by climbing Carn Mor Dearg and Ben Nevis as an excursion from the route. But today's destination is Fort William, the finishing point of the Highland High Way. You will be constantly reminded of that as you walk north from Kinlochleven. Fort William is spread out ahead of you soon after you reach the ridge. The town itself, though, is overshadowed by the spectacular views of Ben Nevis, Carn Mor Dearg and the sweeping curve of the arête between them.

The first part of the route covers the same ground as Excursion 3, but the Mamores are a spectacular group of hills and you will relish all the time you spend in them. Today's route completes the traverse of the main ridge started on yesterday's excursion. If you do both, you will have climbed seven of the range's eleven Munros – and you could boost that tally by taking in some of the detours suggested on the Mamores excursion and today's route.

Stob Ban on its own would make today's route worth while. It is an impressive hill. The steep ridges of Coire Mhusgain look like giant arms hugging the steep northern wall below Stob Ban's summit as if trying to keep itself aloof from the other peaks around it. That impression is enhanced by the glitter of its quartzite peak which gives it the name 'white peak'. Unlike many other mountain features, the Coire Mhusgain is no less impressive from close quarters than from a distance – as you will see when you stand on the rim of the corrie later today.

Stob Ban is not today's only attraction. First comes Sgorr an Iubhair, often climbed as part of the traverse of the Devil's Ridge but no less worthy for that. The last of the day's hills, Mullach nan Coirean, confirms that the smallest peaks often have the best views. The most westerly of the Mamores, views from Mullach to its larger neighbours are out-standing. A constant companion on all three peaks will be the enormous granite back of Ben Nevis looming across Glen Nevis.

The Ben's north-eastern face may have the monopoly on the buttresses and gullies which make it so attractive to mountaineers, but the impervious bulk of its massive western wall, seen to great advantage from Mullach's summit, easily identifies it as Britain's highest mountain. Its size is obvious even when, as is all too often, its top is shrouded in cloud.

There is little sign of these delights as you set off from Kinlochleven. The steepness of the Mamores' slopes and the long curve of the ridge directly above the town mean that most of the peaks are hidden from view until you reach the ridge. As with yesterday's excursion, the excellent stalkers' paths make the ascent fast and straightforward. The well-built paths help you forget the fact that, unlike in Glen Coe, the ascent starts from sea-level. Indeed, Sgorr an Iubhair is a contender for the fastest Munro ascent on the route.

The route starts on the West Highland Way which leaves Kinlochleven opposite the school on the north side of the town. The path winds steeply through delightful woodlands of birch, rowan and beech trees. These owe their existence to the aluminium smelter. Employment at the factory was an alternative to sheep-farming, the mainstay of much of the rest of the Highlands even in the late

The rock marking the place to cross the burn

nineteenth century, so the common grazing above the town was little used. That allowed the trees to establish themselves. Elsewhere in the Highlands, any shoots were immediately snapped up by sheep or deer, which partly explains the wide barren areas around many settlements today.

Climb through the trees and cross the tarmac road which leads to the Mamore Lodge, continuing on along the forest track. The trees peter out just as you reach a landrover track winding around the side of the hill. The views across Loch Leven to the Pap of Glencoe and beyond are spectacular, especially in the early-morning light. Turn left along the landrover track through the Lairigmor, the glacier-cleared pass which leads into Fort William. Leave the landrover track after ten minutes and follow a path which climbs to the right just after the track crosses the Eirghe burn on a metal-railed bridge.

The path climbs steeply initially past a series of small waterfalls, then eases as it winds its way up the corrie towards the ridge. It stays on the left-hand side of the burn until halfway up. The crossing point is easy to miss as a variety of small paths carry on up the left of the burn before disappearing completely. The crossing point is at a level spot in the burn, about 200m beyond a large square rock, set on its own pedestal, to the left of the path. It may be difficult to find a clear path immediately after crossing the burn but it becomes obvious again after 100m or so.

The path crosses some smaller burns feeding the Eirghe then swings briefly north-west. It then climbs east towards the summit of Am Bodach and finally north to the ridge. Two cairns, one close to the end of the path and the other on the ridge proper, mark the point where it joins the ridge just as it starts the climb up to Sgur an Iubhair.

If you did not do yesterday's excursion, you may like to add Am Bodach to your Munro tally. It is a quick climb from here – an hour should get you there and back, and you will miss the rough scrambling on the ascent from the eastern side.

To continue today's route, go left along the ridge path. The grassy slopes become steeper and rockier as they approach the summit of Sgorr an Iubhair. The climb from the ridge will take less than 30 minutes. From there, you can gaze in anticipation at the rugged form of Stob Ban in the west. You also get your first views of Fort William in the distance at the end of Glen Nevis. Don't be fooled by the view of the journey's end – it is likely to take six hours to get there on the day's circuitous but pleasant route. On its top, you may also ponder how Sgorr an Iubhair got its name, 'peak of the yew', for you would have to descend a long way to find any tree at all, let alone a yew.

The summit is a fine spot for contemplating the Devil's Ridge to Sgurr a' Mhaim. It is the narrowest of all the Mamores' ridge-walks, emphasised by the Scottish Mountaineering Club guide's warning that 'inexperienced climbers might welcome a rope'. The guide relates the story of a traverse by climbing pioneer William Inglis Clark in 1880. He had to lift his companion – who, admittedly, was poorly shod in smooth leather-soled shoes – by the collar across the narrowest section. The offending part is easily identifiable about halfway along to the Sgurr a' Mhaim summit. For all the guide's warnings, the walk is a rewarding one and, in good conditions, relatively straightforward. It is an alternative way into Fort William should you find Sgurr a' Mhaim a more tempting prospect than Stob Ban, although the walk through Glen Nevis is long and, especially in the summer months, busy with traffic.

To continue along the route to Stob Ban, go north from the summit to the col between Sgorr an Iubhair and Sgurr a' Mhaim. The well-worn path is quite steep. At the col, instead of taking the more obvious northern path towards the Devil's Ridge, head south-west down a series of zigzags to a small tear-shaped lochan, Lochan Coire Nam Miseach, which lies at the base of the sheer wall below Sgorr an Iubhair.

The lochan is a delightful spot to stop for refreshment. Perched between Sgurr a' Mhaim and Stob Ban, the views are excellent. From here you will be able to see Ben Nevis and the tree-lined glen below it winding its way down towards Fort

Stob Ban

William. A spring just behind the lochan provides deliciously cool water at virtually all times of the year. The barking call of ravens is sometimes heard as they fly around the hills. Ptarmigans and snow bunting are also common, and even the more elusive birds of prey like golden eagles or peregrine falcons may be spotted circling high above.

From the lochan, the path climbs gently west to the grassy slopes of the ridge. About 300m beyond the lochan a cairn marks a path on the right which heads down to Poldubh and then, via Glen Nevis, into Fort William, should weather or lack of energy deter you from continuing along the ridge. The path to Stob Ban becomes more bouldery and then steepens dramatically into a rocky scramble just below its summit. There are plenty of foot- and handholds, and the ascent is not difficult.

As you approach the summit, you get a close-up view of the cavernous Coire Mhusgain plunging dramatically to the glen below. The path on to the summit winds close enough to the edge of the corrie to allow you to appreciate its steep wall and vertical drops.

From the summit of Stob Ban, Mullach nan Coirean looks just a step away across the appropriately named Coire Dearg, 'red corrie'. But the ridge along to it weaves in a series of curves, so the journey time of one-and-a-half to two hours is longer than you might expect. The clear path heads north from Stob Ban's summit across a field of shattered quartz boulders, then climbs to a top where a small cairn marks the transition from boulderfield to grassier slopes. The path turns north-west then west on its winding route to Mullach nan Coirean.

A line of boulders crosses the ridge and stretches for miles up one side of the hill and down the other. It marks the path of an old wall – a reminder of the importance that was attached to grazing land in the Highlands. Notice also the changing geology of the hill, as the sharp quartzite is replaced by the granite which gives Mullach nan Coirean its distinctive red glow. The transition is also marked by an increase in vegetation.

The path eventually heads north-west, widening out from a narrow ridge to a grassy slope. Loch Leven, which can still be seen glinting in the glen below, may not have as many islands as Loch Lomond, but those it has have no less interesting a history. The largest, at the mouth of the loch, is Eilean Munde, named after St Fintan Mundus who built a church on the island. It was the burial-ground of three clans, the MacDonalds of Glen Coe, the Stewarts of Balluchulish and the Camerons of Callert. All used different landing-places, called 'ports of the dead', and would return to shore rather than land on the island if one of the other clans was already conducting a burial. It was the burial place of MacIain, chief of the MacDonald clan who was killed in the massacre of Glen Coe. Another grave-stone carries the warning:

> *My glass has run*
> *Yours is running*
> *Be warned in time*
> *Your hour is coming.*

A neighbouring island, Eilean a' Chomhraidh, 'isle of discussion', was the place for settling clan disputes. When an agreement was reached, it was signed on the Eilean na Bainne, 'isle of covenant', close by.

Ahead on the ridge, a clear top, marked with a sizeable cairn, could easily be confused with the summit on a cloudy day. The imposter will quickly be unmasked when you reach the real summit. Mullach's broad, bouldery top is marked by the largest cairn of the whole route, making it look as if its fans are trying to make up for the fact that it is lower than its westerly and northerly neighbours.

As its name – 'peak of the corries' – indicates, Mullach nan Coirean has its share of corries too. Four of them swoop away to the north, south, east

Sgurr a' Mhaim and the Devil's Ridge

and north-west, although none is as dramatic as Stob Ban's Coire Mhusgain. Nor are they craggy enough to break Mullach's round, easy angles – a feature which will be appreciated on the descent into Glen Nevis.

Mullach nan Coirean's summit may be a feature-less boulderfield, but the splendid views to its higher neighbours make it well worth lingering a while. As well as the now familiar Mamores and Ben Nevis, you can look back to the Aonach Eagach, which seems benign from this distance, with the mass of Bidean nam Bian looming above it. In the south-west your eye will be drawn to the glittering water of Loch Linnhe, a delightful foreground for the hills

of the Ardgour peninsula beyond.

To begin the descent into Glen Nevis, head along Mullach's north ridge. A path comes and goes amid grassy slopes, interspersed with rocks and crags. Make sure you do not follow the path on the north-east shoulder, as this descends high up in Glen Nevis and means a long walk down into Fort William.

After 40 minutes' walking along the ridge, the buildings of the Blarmachfoldach farm appear in the north-west. Head down the slope towards them and a gap in the forest at the foot of the slope will soon come into view. Carrying on further down the ridge towards the outcrop of Sgorr Chalum may seem more direct, but this involves picking a path over burns and across broken and rocky ground, and so is not recommended.

The descent is steep but the slopes are grassy so the going is not difficult. The short distance across the glen is fairly dry, and the heather and azalea bushes not too dense. As you descend, the view south-west to the little Lochan Lunn Da Bhra, at the head of the Lairigmor, is delightful.

In poor visibility the forests can be found by walking along the ridge for 30 to 40 minutes from the summit then heading north-west.

On reaching the path between the two plantations turn right and climb the stile to enter the forest and head to Fort William. The denseness of the Forestry Commission plantation contrasts sharply with this morning's walk through the forest above Kinloch-leven. This plantation is thick and monotonous, despite attempts to vary the uniformity with a few indigenous trees scattered along the side of the path. The vegetation also becomes less mountainous with foxgloves and other plants associated with lower altitudes joining the heathers and mosses.

Walking on the path is easy; given that Fort William is still two hours away, this is much appreciated. As you descend through the forest, a sign invites you to take a detour to Dun Deardil, site of an ancient vitrified fort, dating back to the Iron Age.

The path gradually widens to a forestry track amid an area devastated by tree-clearing. Looking back-wards, there are excellent views to the Mamores. The youth hostel lies two miles out of town, across the road from the start of the route up Ben Nevis, and there are campsites along the road into Fort William.

The town has a variety of hotels, guest houses and bed & breakfasts. It is worth choosing accommodation as close as possible to the path up Ben Nevis from Glen Nevis to avoid lengthening tomorrow's walk, if you intend doing the final excursion. Reaching Fort William also means you will have access to a range of amenities like pharmacies, cash machines, pizza parlours and an Indian restaurant, and banks with normal opening hours for the first time since Drymen.

The town of Fort William started as a fort built by General Monck between 1649 and 1660 on the instructions of Oliver Cromwell who wanted to control the unruly Highlanders. It was then called Inverlochy but the name was changed to Fort William, after William III, who had it reconstructed in 1690. It survived Jacobite sieges in both the 1715 and 1745 rebellions but was finally dismantled in 1894, not by Highlanders or other marauders but to make way for the West Highland Railway.

Courtesy of that railway and its position under Ben Nevis and at the end of the Great Glen, Fort William is the unofficial capital of the western Highlands. Among other things, that means lots of tourists. Judging by the numbers which swarm around the town whatever the time of year, few would agree with Frank Fraser Darling, the famous Scottish naturalist. In his *West Highland Survey*, he described Fort William as 'an eyesore. The excessive rainfall and the deep shade cast by Ben Nevis and the lesser hills restrict the sunshine still further.' As he also points out, however, the attractions of the hills and glens more than make up for the failings of the town. With that, at least, few could disagree.

The bars, restaurants and hotels give you a choice of ways to celebrate your completion of the Highland High Way. You may, however, prefer to save your celebration until after the grand finale – the ascent of Ben Nevis.

USEFUL INFORMATION

Accommodation: Numerous hotel and guest houses. For details contact the Tourist Information Office, 01397 660068

Youth Hostel: Glen Nevis Youth Hostel, 01397 702336

Bunkhouse: Achintee farm, 01397 702240

Transport: Bus to Glasgow, 0990 505050
Train to Glasgow, 01397 703791

Supplies: A full range of shops and services

Bank: Several branches of banks and building societies

Stalking: British Alcan Aluminium, 01397 702433

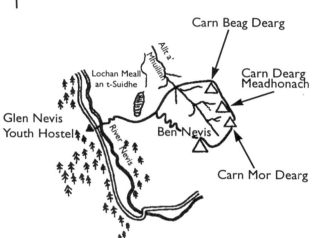

Carn Beag Dearg

Carn Dearg
Meadhonach

Carn Mor Dearg

Alt a' Mhuilinn

Lochan Meall
an t-Suidhe

Glen Nevis
Youth Hostel

River Nevis

Ben Nevis

Excursion 4

Ben Nevis

Excursion 4
Ben Nevis

ROUTE SUMMARY

Climb the path from the Glen Nevis youth hostel to Lochan Meall an t-Suidhe. Leave the path there and go north then east to cross the Allt a' Mhuilinn and climb Carn Beag Dearg. Follow the ridge over Carn Dearg Meadhonach to Carn Mor Dearg. Traverse the arête south and south-west and then climb to Ben Nevis's summit. Descend east on the tourist path to Glen Nevis.

Distance: 18km
Time: 8hr 30min
Ascent: 1,674m
Descent: 1,674m

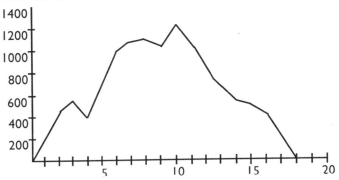

Ben Nevis is Britain's highest and most popular mountain, as will be obvious should you climb it on a fine summer's day. On the early part of the route you may be accompanied by hordes of day-trippers struggling up the steep path to the summit in everything from flip-flops to wellington boots. Do not be too disheartened. The Highland High Way route to Ben Nevis via Carn Mor Dearg and its exhilarating arête bears no relation to the tourist path. From Carn Mor Dearg, you will have a grandstand view of the Ben's massive buttresses, gullies and pillars; the tourists will see only its whale back. You will enjoy tackling the longest arête on mainland Britain; they will toil up an interminable zigzagging path in the company of wailing infants, panting parents and groaning grannies. They may wonder why they bothered once they reach the debris-strewn summit; you will have the satisfaction of a dramatic ascent which makes it all worth while.

Tourists are not the only hazard on the Ben Nevis path. The numbers slogging up with sofas, wheelbarrows, pianos and the like rise and fall with the popularity of sponsored fundraising. But super-fit runners are a regular sight particularly as the Annual Ben Nevis Race, held on the first Saturday of September, approaches. You may wonder about the sanity of someone who chooses to race up Britain's highest mountain, but you cannot deny their achievement. The record time, set in 1984, is 1 hour, 25 minutes and 34 seconds from Fort William to the summit and back – about the time it will take you to reach the Allt a' Mhuilinn.

The Highland High Way does not avoid the tourist path completely – although you could easily do that if you start in the north of the town and walk to the path which runs up from behind the distillery on the A82. Be warned though: the lower reaches of this are almost always boggy and you are likely to get your feet wet. If you start at the distillery, you will join today's route at the foot of Carn Beag Dearg.

The ascent from the youth hostel zigzags on a clear path up the Ben's lower slopes. Those who are staying in the town can take the path which starts at the parking area in front of Achintee farm a mile closer to Fort William. That ascends gradually round the slopes of Meall an t-Suidhe and joins the path from the youth hostel after half an hour's walking. Wherever you set off from, you are advised to start as early as possible both to beat the rush and because, at eight to ten hours, this is one of the longest days of the Highland High Way.

Forty-five minutes after leaving the youth hostel a path branches left as the Lochan Meall an t-Suidhe comes into view in the west. Ignore the wall of stones on the bend of the zigzag, designed to ensure that the tourists don't stray off their path, and head north. The lochan is delightful, particularly in still weather when it reflects the colours of the hills and sky all around. It makes an ideal spot for rough camping but make sure you remove all traces of your stay when you leave.

The tourist track climbs 600m relatively quickly but some of that height will be lost as you cross the Allt a' Mhuilinn to climb Carn Beag Dearg. Descend north-east to the burn as it comes into view. It is easier to cross further downstream if the water is high. You may be tempted to avoid the drop by following the path round Castle Ridge, which goes to the Charles Inglis Clark hut in Coire Leis; but the further up the corrie you go, the steeper and stonier Carn Mor Dearg's western slopes become. Crossing the burn at the mouth of the corrie and climbing to Carn Beag Dearg may be less direct, but the ascent is less difficult.

This is not to say that this route is easy. Having crossed to the other side of the burn it is a long, calf-aching slog to the ridge joining the three Carn Dearg summits. Aiming directly for the first of them, Carn Beag Dearg, gives the best going. That means heading east up the slope (or slightly to the south of east if you had to go downstream to cross the burn). It will come as a relief to reach the first summit, particularly as you will have anticipated the goal many times before you actually reach it. Even more welcome is the easy walk up to Carn Mor Dearg from here, giving plenty of time to admire the awesome glory of Ben Nevis across Coire Leis.

And awesome it certainly is. Even those who never intend to climb a sheer cliff-face will enjoy trying to pick out the famous climbing routes, like Lobby Dancer which runs from the terrace halfway up the most northerly buttress, Castle Ridge; Glover's Chimney on Tower Ridge, the other arm of Coire na Ciste; and Rubicon Wall on the eastern face of the Observatory Ridge which plunges from the summit plateau. The only sign of mountaineers on any of these climbs is likely to be their voices, calling instructions and signals to each other. Actually picking them out on the massive walls is more or less impossible.

Ben Nevis was not officially crowned king of the mountains until 1847, when Ordnance Survey measurements finally ended the claim of Ben Macdui in the Cairngorms, a full 35m lower. The derivation of Ben Nevis's name is uncertain. W.H. Murray suggest it comes from the Gaelic *Beinn-neamh-bhathais*, meaning 'mountain with its head in the clouds'. The more common translation is 'hill of poison or venom', from *Beinn Nimheis*. Given the weather and the number of accidents on the mountain both translations are appropriate.

The first ascent of Ben Nevis is not recorded. James Robertson is known to have reached the top in 1771, in search of botanical specimens for his museum, and there are other accounts of climbs in the early eighteenth century. The accolade of the first climb without a guide goes to William Naismith, famed for his useful rule used to estimate journey times in the hills.

The long slog to the ridge will remind you that Carn Mor Dearg is a serious hill in its own right. But for the lure of its larger neighbour, perhaps more walkers would decide to savour the ridge and climb its conical summit to admire the stunning views of the Mamores in the south, not to mention those of the Ben itself. Their loss is your gain; enjoy the glorious spectacle in peace.

Carn Mor Dearg is just 124m lower than Ben Nevis, making it Britain's seventh-highest peak, as well as the second-highest on our route. Indeed, Carn Dearg Meadhonach, at 1,179m, is the third-highest point reached on the Highland High Way, although it does not even merit the status of a top in Munro's tables. Even Carn Beag Dearg's 1,010m make it a decent conquest in its own right.

All this makes today a serious day's walking. The

Carn Mor Dearg arête

thousands of people slogging up the tourist path close by does not mean these hills can be taken lightly. Snow lies on both Ben Nevis and Carn Mor Dearg long after it has disappeared from lesser hills – even the hottest August for decades failed to dislodge patches of snow lingering in Gardyloo and Tower gullies – and winds of 100 miles an hour are not unknown on the mountain.

The height of these mountains means that, more often than not, they are shrouded in cloud and mist. It is vital that you are confident of your ability to navigate in snow and poor visibility. This particularly important on Ben Nevis itself, where the dual hazards of Gardyloo and Five Finger Gully lurk at either edge of the summit plateau. Ben Nevis is the site of more fatal accidents than any other Scottish mountain.

From the summit of Carn Beag Dearg, a path comes and goes as the ridge winds along to Carn Dearg Meadhonach and Carn Mor Dearg itself. These translate, appropriately if unimaginatively, as 'small red hill', 'middle red hill' and 'big red hill' respectively. Red will seem a very apt description when you look back on the hill from the summit of Ben Nevis.

It is a testament to the dramatic way the Carn Mor Dearg arête swoops across the top of Coire Leis that it is not overshadowed by the Ben's buttresses and gullies. From here, the arête looks even more spectacular than it did from the Mamores to the south. The longest part, directly below the boulderfield which climbs to Ben Nevis's summit, grows in stature as you head along the ridge. The southern spur, which comes into view only as you reach the summit of Carn Mor Dearg, is if anything sharper and more precipitous.

The sharpness of the arête contrasts with the smooth, wide slope of the aptly named Aonach Mor, 'long ridge', across the glen to the east. Now the site of a ski centre, the workings of the chairlift can be seen on the northern slope – small wonder, therefore, that most walkers choose to avoid the ski paraphernalia and reach that summit from Glen Nevis.

As you reach the summit of Carn Dearg Meadhonach, the Mamores ridge appears beyond the arête. This is the best angle from which to admire the steep northern face of Am Bodach. Stob Ban and Sgurr a' Mhaim still shine out as the stars of the Mamores. The drop from the arête to Coire Leis looks unnervingly steep from this angle. What you cannot see from here is the path on the other side which helps vertigo-sufferers avoid the airiest parts of the ridge.

From Carn Dearg Meadhonach the summit cairn of Carn Mor Dearg can be seen. Approaching it, the contrast between its cone and the glowering hulk of Ben Nevis becomes even more obvious – a clear sign of their different geology. Like Glencoe, Ben Nevis is a legacy of ancient volcanic eruptions. But, while Glen Coe was the result of a ring fault which sank immediately into a pool of lava below, Ben Nevis is the remainder of a massive plug of lava which stopped the top of an enormous chasm below it. The chasm gradually filled with magma and, when the plug eventually sank, it was baked to impervious andesite which is more resistant to weathering than the softer rocks around it. They, like Ben Nevis's lower slopes, are mainly of granite – as is clear from the pink boulders strewn over Carn Mor Dearg's summits – which were long ago stripped of their lava covering by weathering and glacial erosion.

Ben Nevis's geology, as well as its height and bad weather, explains the lack of vegetation on the higher slopes. While most of the hills on the route have managed to sustain some heathers, myrtle and

On the arête

mosses, the boulder slopes around the Ben's summit
are almost completely barren.

The arête starts immediately below the summit of
Carn Mor Dearg. To reach it head south, ignoring a
path to the east which goes down to Glen Nevis via

the impressive Coire Giubhsachan. The path along the arête lies just below the ridge for most of its length. It starts on the Coire Leis side then crosses to the south side as the arête curves around the top of the corrie. The initial part of the arête, before it turns south-west at the tower about a third of the way along its length, is likely to take longest as you will have to constantly clamber up and down to find the best route. Where there is no obvious path, keeping to the highest point gives the easiest, and least scary, route except in high winds, when the top of the ridge is too exposed.

This is the longest and narrowest arête on the Highland High Way, but in good weather it presents no difficulty. In snow, wind or rain, however, it requires more care and must not be taken lightly. It takes longer to cross than you might think – up to two hours to traverse its length. The arête is higher than it looks from Carn Mor Dearg, falling to just 1,058m at its lowest point, although that still leaves almost 300m of climbing to the summit of Ben Nevis. It is an exciting scramble, an excellent way to approach Britain's highest hill and a fitting challenge for the final excursion of the Highland High Way. You should take time to savour it; it may prove far more satisfying than the conquest of the Ben itself.

The end of the arête is marked by a post and a sign identifying the place to abseil down into Coire Leis. The final hurdle on the ascent is the boulderfield which lies directly below Ben Nevis's summit. Although it is the longest and steepest of all the boulderfields on the Highland High Way, in good visibility it is not a difficult climb. From the abseiling pole go first west then north-west to the summit. A path is discernible close to the edge of Coire Leis for much of the route, but erosion and scree on this path makes it easier to pick your way from boulder to boulder.

This ascent can be very dangerous in winter. In poor visibility you should make use of the line of poles on the boulderfield, intended as winter markers to keep climbers away from the large cornices which can overhang the corrie. You must take extreme care in snowy conditions as the slip of an ice-axe could mean you slide straight down into the jaws of Coire Leis.

Excitement at reaching the top of the boulderfield is soon replaced by surprise at finding yourself on the edge of a wide plateau, so strewn with rubble and debris it looks as if it has just been hit by a hurricane. In contrast with the narrow summit plateaux of Carn Mor Dearg and the hills of Glen Coe and the Mamores, the top of Ben Nevis is a battlefield, strewn not just with rocks and boulders, but with commemorative cairns and plaques, shelters and viewfinders and the remnants of the observatory and hotel which were once open here.

On a clear day the views are as extensive as you would expect from the highest point in Britain. Ben Lawers and Schiehallion in the south-east, the Paps of Jura to the south-west, the Cuillins on Skye in the west and the Cairngorms in the east are all visible when the light is good. You may be able to make out Ireland and the Ochil hills to the north of Glasgow if the weather is clear enough. Arguing about which peak is which should keep you occupied for most of your time on the summit and distract you from the debris strewn all around.

While your first instinct may be to head straight back down the way you came, it is worth examining the relics on the summit for the stories they tell about Britain's biggest hill. Prominent among the debris is the ruined observatory, which sent hourly weather reports by telegraph to Fort William for 20 years from October 1883. Its existence was a tribute to the efforts of Clement L. Wragge (dubbed the Inclement Wragge by the newspapers of the time). He climbed to the summit at 4 a.m. each day for five months in the summers of 1881 and 1882 to collect enough data to persuade the authorities of the value of an observatory on the summit.

William T. Kilgour, in his book *Twenty Years on Ben Nevis*, gave the best account of what it is like to live 1,344m above sea-level. As well as the expected weather observations (over six metres of rain in 1898, average temperatures below freezing and gales of up to 150 miles an hour), he also records how uncomfortable it was when things went wrong. The tourist path was created as a pony track to service the observatory but its existence did not make house calls any more attractive to doctors. They twice had to come out 'at great personal risk' to tend to a cook with rheumatic fever. Nor can the sick man's descent have been particularly pleasant, swathed in blankets strapped to the back of a pony.

Kilgour's account of dealing with toothache is enough to make strong men cringe: 'From the tool box to the medicine chest. First a pair of pliers, then a cocaine lotion, followed alternately by a mustard plaster, a concoction of salt and brandy, a mouthful of snow, an Irish jig and lastly, if all these failed, a strenuous endeavour to kill the nerve by prodding

The final ascent on the Highland High Way

the offending molar with a needle.'

His book was published in the hope of gaining enough public sympathy to get the observatory reopened, but to no avail. An early attempt to attract tourists to the summit with the opening of Britain's highest hotel was scarcely more successful. Those first tourists could not reward themselves with a celebratory drink – it was a Temperance hotel. But, the 1894 Fort William tourist guide records, it did offer 'sleeping accommodation for over a dozen guests where tea and bed and breakfast may be obtained for half-a-guinea – a small sum to pay for the proud boast in future years that you have slept on the summit of Ben Nevis.' The hotel survived until the First World War, when it fell into disuse and was never reopened.

That early travel book also cautions travellers not to attempt the climb without a guide as 'mists descend on the summit without a minute's warning and render the position of the climber extremely dangerous'.

Sound advice to this day. No matter how careful you are, in poor visibility it is all too easy to stray accidentally into one of the gullies which lurk at the edge of the summit plateau. That makes it essential to follow the bad-visibility instructions from the summit, given opposite. Holding the course will be difficult in driving wind, snow or rain. Its effectiveness depends on your ability to set a compass bearing accurately.

In good weather the route west off the summit will be obvious. While you may be tempted to take one of the steeper paths down, marking the original pony track route, these are badly eroded and are slower and more dangerous than following the wide zigzags down. Construction of the path at the time the observatory was opened cost £800 and, in the early years of its use, walkers were expected to contribute a shilling to its upkeep, receiving in exchange a card, stamped 'Ben Nevis summit', with the date when they reached the top.

The spectacular views across Loch Linnhe to Skye

and beyond from the path will speed you down the hill. The path is well laid and clear enough to ensure you can stroll down easily to the youth hostel, leaving plenty of time to reflect on today's conquest and your achievement in completing the Highland High Way. You can now look forward to a celebratory drink when you reach Fort William. You have earned it.

Stalking: British Alcan Aluminium, 01397 702433

Bad weather descent from Ben Nevis
From the trig point go 150m on grid bearing 231 degrees. Turn and follow a grid bearing 281 degrees off the summit plateau.

In 1995 magnetic north was 5 degrees west of grid north. Add this to the grid bearing for the compass bearing.

Appendix 1
Glossary of Gaelic Names

This is a brief glossary of the main hills crossed on the route and some of the features seen on the mountain. It also gives pronunciations where they are not obvious. For more detailed study, Ordnance Survey publish a booklet, *Placenames on Maps of Scotland and Wales*. The Scottish Mountaineering Trust book, *Scottish Hill and Mountain Names*, by Peter Drummond, is also useful.

allt	burn or river	
Am Bodach	the old man	
An Caisteal	the castle	*an casteal*
Aonach Eagach	notched ridge	*oenach aykach*
beag/beg	small	*beck*
bealach	pass or col	*byealach*
ben	hill or mountain	
beinn	hill or mountain	*byn*
binnein	pointed hill or peak	*beenyan*
Beinn an Dothaidh	hill of the scorching	*byn an doee*
Beinn Bhreac	speckled hill	*byn vrechk*
Beinn Chabhair	hill of the hawk	*byn chavar*
Beinn Dorain	hill of the streamlet	
Ben Dubhchraig	black rock hill	*byn doochraik*
Ben Lomond	beacon hill	
Ben Lui	hill of the calves	*ben looee*
Ben Nevis	venomous hill	
Ben Oss	hill of the loch outlet	
Ben Vorlich	hill of the sea bay	
brae	slope	
Breac Leac	speckled flat stone	*brech lyech*
Buachaille Etive Mor	big herdsman of the etive	*booachil etiv moar*

buidhe	golden yellow	*booe*
cairn/carn	heap of stones	
Carn Beag Dearg	little red hill	*carn beck jerrack*
Carn Dearg Meadhonach	middle red hill	*carn jerrack meeanach*
Carn Mor Dearg	big red hill	*carn moar jerrack*
Clach Leathad	stone of the broad slope	usually *clachlat*
coille/choille	wood	*chilay*
coire	bowl	*corrie*
creise	origin unknown	*craysh*
croft	small piece of arable land or farm	
Cruinn a Bheinn	round hill	*chroeen a vyn*
dail	flood plain of river	
darach	oak wood	
dearg	red	*jerrack*
dubh	black or dark	*doo*
eag	rocky notch or gap	*ayk*
eas	waterfall	*es*
eilein/eilean	island	
garbh	rough	*garav*
glas	greenish grey	
inver	confluence of waters/ mouth of stream	
lairig	mountain pass	
liath	grey	*leea*
mam	large round hill	
meall	shapeless hill or lump	*myowl*
Meall a' Bhuiridh	hill of the bellowing (of stags)	*myowl a voree*
Meall Dearg	red hill	*myowl jerrack*
mor	big	*moar*
mullach	summit	*mullach*
Mullach nan Coirean	summit of the corries	*mullach nan kooran*
Na Gruagaichean	the maidens	*na grooakeechan*
odhar	dun or yellowish	*oaar*
shieling	settlement	
sgor(r)/sgur(r)	steep hill or crag	*skor/skoor*

Sgorr an Iubhair	peak of the yew	*skor an your-ar*
Sgor Eilde Beag	little peak of the hind	*skor ailta beck*
sron	nose	*srawn*
Sron Garbh	rough jutting peak	*srawn garav*
stob	pointed hill	*stop*
Stob Ban	light-coloured peak	*stop ban*
Stob Coire Altrium	peak of the rearing	*stop corrie altrium*
Stob Coire a'Chairn	peak of the corrie of the cairn	*stop corrie a cairn*
Stob Dearg	red peak	*stop jerrack*
Stob na Doire	peak of the thicket	*stop na dira*
Stob Ghabhar	goat peak	*stop gowar*
tor, torr	rocky outcrop	

Appendix 2
Further Reading

Fiction
Munro, Neil, *John Splendid* (any edition)
Munro, Neil, *The New Road* (any edition)
Macintyre, Duncan Ban, *Beinn Dorain*, trans Iain Crichton Smith (Northern House, 1988)
Scott, Sir Walter, *Rob Roy* (any edition)
Stevenson, Robert Louis, *Kidnapped* (any edition)

General
Breadalbane, Marchioness of, *High Tops of the Black Mount* (Blackwood, 1935)
Darling, F. Fraser, *West Highland Survey* (Oxford University Press, 1955)
Drummond, Peter, *Scottish Hill and Place Names* (Scottish Mountainerring Trust)
Haldane, A. R. B., *The Drove Roads of Scotland* (Edinburgh University Press, 1971)
Kilgour, William T., *Twenty Years on Ben Nevis*
Murray, W. H., *The Scottish Highlands* (Scottish Mountaineering Trust, 1976)
Prebble, John, *Glencoe: The Story of the Massacre* (Penguin, 1966)
Thomas, John, *The West Highland Railway* (Pan, 1970)
Heading for the Scottish Hills (Scottish Mountaineering Trust, 1988)
Munro's Tables (Scottish Mountaineering Trust, 1990)
Placenames on Maps of Scotland and Wales (Ordnance Survey, 1981)
Safety on Mountains (British Mountaineering Council, 1988)
West Highland Way leaflet (Scottish Natural Heritage, Battleby, Redgorton, Perth PH1 3EW, 01738 627921)